More Pr

Burn Your Business Plan!

"David Gumpert has done it again! But this is more than just another superb book. Based on his accumulated wisdom, he has dared challenge the status quo in educating entrepreneurs. Our overemphasis on writing business plans has been exposed--and equally important, he has provided a superior path for the startup entrepreneur."

Gerald E. Hills
Coleman/Denton Thorne Professor of Entrepreneurship and Executive Director
of the Institute for Entrepreneurial Studies
University of Illinois at Chicago

"Gumpert successfully captures a significant shift in the way leading entrepreneurs are launching companies and attracting investors. He emphasizes the areas where many entrepreneurs should be focusing their limited resources--on bootstrapping, executive summaries, financial projections, and the management team. As he suggests, 'fairy tale' plans are out, and entrepreneurs who expect to succeed in this new environment must make major adjustments in the way they develop and present their plans."

John R. Thorne
Morgenthaler Professor of Entrepreneurship
Carnegie Mellon University

"*Burn Your Business Plan!* provides a refreshing, realistic look at the real role of business plans in the founding and growth of a successful business. Unlike the all-too-common 'How To Write A Business Plan' primers, Gumpert provides the reader with a clear understanding of how to successfully plan a new business venture. This is a welcome new paradigm."

Jeffrey Shuman
Professor of Entrepreneurship and Director of the Bentley Center for
Entrepreneurial Studies
Bentley College

"*Burn Your Business Plan!* successfully challenges the status quo on the role of business planning in the entrepreneurial process, and provides an important new approach for attracting financing. I know it will provoke spirited discussions in collegiate entrepreneurship classes around the country."

Elizabeth Gates
Jack M. Gill Chair of Entrepreneurship and Director of the Johnson Center for
Entrepreneurship & Innovation
Kelley School of Business
Indiana University

"A highly engaging and thought-provoking book by a notable business-planning expert--and a breath of fresh air...Gumpert takes entrepreneurs behind the scenes to explain how investors think and make decisions. *Burn Your Business Plan!* is bound to launch a healthy debate about the role of the business plan in raising capital."

Julian Lange
Associate Professor of Entrepreneurship
Babson College

"*Burn Your Business Plan!* is right on target in describing the changed landscape for entrepreneurs preparing to approach investors. It makes the invaluable point that professional investors first and foremost want to understand the individuals behind the business, and hear their visions for the future. In this new mix, the business plan assumes the role of backup in communicating the entrepreneur's thinking, rather than the lead role. I recommend this for all entrepreneurs who are serious about raising money."

Bob Marshall
Managing Partner
Selby Ventures

"Thanks to David for exposing the 'dirty little secret' about attracting investors and acquirers--that most successful companies do it without a business plan. He completes the circle, though, by using clear explanations and great war stories to show the actual techniques these companies use to get the job done."

Michael Gonnerman, financial consultant to growing companies

Burn Your Business Plan!

What Investors *Really* Want from Entrepreneurs

By David E. Gumpert

Burn Your Business Plan!

What Investors *Really* Want from Entrepreneurs

By David E. Gumpert

Copyright © David E. Gumpert, 2002
Published by Lauson Publishing Co., Needham, MA
All Rights Reserved
Printed in the United States of America

ISBN 0-9701181-5-5

Library of Congress Control Number: 2002092517

Preface

How does someone who has written extensively in support of a serious business practice—in this case business planning—come to completely change his viewpoint and approach to the subject? For me, it was the result of observing one too many entrepreneurs commit huge amounts of time and energy to preparing a written business plan in the belief the plan was essential to obtaining investor interest, and then coming up empty.

I realized that the cost to these entrepreneurs extended way beyond their time and energy—that there was a huge opportunity cost as well. The resources that went into producing a business plan could have been directed toward activities that would have been more productive both in attracting investment interest and in improving the odds of business success.

I also realized that the near-automatic advice experts give to entrepreneurs about writing a business plan before doing anything else is a glaring example of how the entrepreneurial process is misrepresented and twisted by various important institutions in our society, such as the media, major corporations, and even business schools. Part of the problem is that entrepreneurship has become overly glamorized in our culture. Particularly successful entrepreneurs are portrayed as celebrities. People like Bill Gates and Michael Dell are held up as examples of what is possible, with the implication that anyone can do what they did, if the individuals just plan and persevere. The reality is that most people can never achieve what these and other especially accomplished entrepreneurs achieved, whether for lack of talent, inopportune timing, or inappropriate product. Different approaches work for different people

The hype that surrounds the traditional business plan won't end easily, however. If anything, the promotion has become more intense into the early 2000s, as even the most prestigious universities in the country, such as Harvard and MIT, now use "business plan contests" as pretexts to garner publicity for themselves and attract financial contributions and student applications. The tail is ever more wagging the dog.

It isn't enough merely to argue that an approach is wrong. It's important to provide an alternative path. I have tried to do that here, suggesting a more flexible approach that allows entrepreneurs to build their businesses in ways that are more likely to attract investment. It's important that would-be and existing entrepreneurs learn to follow their passions, and discover what works for them as well as the marketplace.

--David E. Gumpert

About the Author

David E. Gumpert is author or co-author of seven books on various aspects of business, including the best-selling *How to Really Create a Successful Business Plan* (Inc. Publishing) and *Business Plans That Win $$$: Lessons from the MIT Enterprise Forum* (with Stanley Rich), published by HarperCollins

He co-founded a successful Internet direct marketing agency in 1995 that grew to twenty employees and was acquired by a publicly-held company in 1999. He has consulted with dozens of entrepreneurs about their growth plans, and has spoken to entrepreneurship and trade organizations as well as business students about business planning issues.

Prior to his entrepreneurship career, Gumpert was a journalist, serving nine years as a staff reporter with *The Wall Street Journal* and seven years as small business editor of the *Harvard Business Review*. He was also a senior editor of *Inc.* Magazine.

Gumpert is a graduate of the University of Chicago and the Columbia University Graduate School of Journalism.

He is currently president of Gumpert Communications Inc. of Needham, MA, which specializes in providing specialized communications and consulting services to growing companies. He can be contacted via email, david@gumpertcom.com.

For my wife, Jean

Table of Contents

Acknowledgments

I 've been very fortunate to have had the support of a wide variety of individuals—entrepreneurs, academics, venture capitalists, consultants, and editorial experts—as I've pushed to complete this book. I'm always moved when individuals who have nothing overtly to gain are so generous in sharing their expertise, in the interests of helping entrepreneurs avoid errors and blind alleys.

First, I want to thank the 42 venture capitalists around the country who agreed to answer my survey questions about their investment decision-making processes. While I promised them anonymity in exchange for their candid responses, I recognize that they are from important and influential firms, and thus have many activities competing for their limited time.

Several entrepreneurs were also very giving. Jonathan Carson, a founder of Family Education Network (FEN) of Boston, which was sold to Pearson in 2000 for $175 million, went so far as to write a detailed account of his experiences raising more than $50 million of investment funds, as part of Chapter 12. Steve Snyder, a founder of Centerstone Software of Westwood, MA, shared a highly productive synopsis he sent to prospective investors, which helped Centerstone raise more than $4 million.

I am grateful to Michael Gonnerman, a financial consultant and former advisory board member of a company I co-founded, for sharing sample financial projection documents he has assembled, and for reviewing an early version of this book. Mike is a clear thinker who loves to guide entrepreneurs through the thicket of problems they face, and has gone so far as to make much essential

information available on his Web site,
www.gonnerman.com.

A serial entrepreneur and founder of a Boston-area
entrepreneurs' forum, Peter Schmidt, also took the time to
review my manuscript, and via his inputs shared the
perspective of an entrepreneur who has negotiated
extensively with professional investors. Larry Adolf, a
partner at Emigrant Capital, provided invaluable criticisms
of my manuscript from the investor perspective.

On the academic side, I have been fortunate to be
able to pick the brains of such luminaries in the teaching of
entrepreneurship as Jeffry Timmons and Julian Lange of
Babson College, Jerry Katz of Saint Louis University, and
Jeffrey Shuman of Bentley College. Julian and Jerry
reviewed the manuscript and provided valuable insights. Jeff
Shuman went so far as to allow me to try some of my ideas
on one of his classes on business planning, and I credit his
students with helping me refine some of the book's ideas.

Several editorial experts and colleagues have also
provided important input and support. Barry Neville, a
talented editor at McGraw-Hill Trade, provided the
inspiration that led to the book's title. Patti Abbate helped
edit the manuscript and prepare it for production. Rob
Parmenter helped put together chapter summaries, and
provided editorial input as well. And Lee Corbin, a
Providence, RI, graphic designer, has shared his amazing
talents in developing the book's cover.

And as usual, members of my family—my wife Jean,
my daughter Laura, and my son Jason—served as important
sounding boards for many of the original ideas behind this
book, in addition to providing essential moral support.

Introduction

Investor Relations for Entrepreneurs

"The bottom line is to understand that I invest in people, not in paper."
—Venture capitalist participant in survey for this book

T his book is intended as an investor relations
guidebook for entrepreneurs.
What does investor relations have to do with entrepreneurs
who may have neither investors, nor relations with investors?
Whether you are seeking millions of dollars of financing
from nationally known venture capital firms or whether you
just want a few hundred dollars of credit from a supplier, you
are engaged in investor relations. In either case, you must
convince outsiders to take a chance on you, to invest in you.

Obviously, it's the financing type of investment that
is of greatest concern for many entrepreneurs, simply
because it is at once so important and so difficult to come by
in our current "age of high anxiety." The United States and,
indeed, much of the world, became enmeshed in an
economic malaise after the blowoff of the dot-com era in
early 2000, and it was only exacerbated by the terrorism
events of September 11, 2001.

Historically, periods of layoffs and high unemployment have been fertile times for entrepreneurship. Individuals who lose their jobs and have trouble finding another often begin to entertain more seriously the common fantasy of going into business for themselves. When these individuals set up shop, and begin shopping for investment funds—often with remarkably creative and viable business concepts—they typically run smack into the harsh reality that investors aren't very forthcoming.

During the post-dot-com era, the climate for investment funds cooled considerably. As one indication, the amount of venture capital funds invested declined more than 50% in just one year, to $36.5 billion in 2001, after increasing more than eight times between 1996 and 2000 (from $9.6 billion to $85.5 billion), according to the MoneyTree Survey, sponsored by Price Waterhouse Coopers, Venture Economics, and the National Venture Capital Association. So many professional investors were so badly burned by the blowoff that they will be nursing their wounds for many years, and are thus much more nervous about making new investments than they were during the 1990s.

Still and all, there is and will continue to be money available for investment—many billions of dollars not only of venture capital, but of so-called "informal capital" that comes from relatives, friends, and "angels". The Ewing Marion Kauffman Foundation, which promotes entrepreneurship, reported that in 2001 angels invested nearly $130 billion in new and young enterprises. There is just too much innovation going on in our society, and resulting opportunities for investment. The tempo of innovation—in biotechnology, telecommunications, security, robotics, and other areas—is too well established to be shut down by cyclical economic cycles. Your job is not only to find the sources of money, but also to shake it loose.

Key to shaking the money loose is understanding the new investment landscape, and how you need to navigate in that landscape. This new landscape is best understood as contrasted to the investment landscape of the previous two decades. The investment process has evolved, influenced by a combination of factors—economic, technological, and cyclical. In the 1980s and into the early 1990s, prospective investors couldn't obtain background information about a company by simply calling up its Web site. Nor had investors previously been as badly burned as they were by the dot-com blowoff. Innovation and change weren't happening as quickly. In that more predictable environment, a written business plan was, as stated in my two previous books about business planning, the "ticket of admission" to the investment process. No business plan, no discussions or negotiations with venture capitalists.

How does all this play itself out in real life? Most fundamentally, the old rules—under which writing a business plan was considered by entrepreneurs to be nearly synonymous with raising money—are quickly giving way to a new approach in which the written business plan has much less prominence, having been replaced by other means of inspiring confidence in tentative investors.

In the traditional approach, entrepreneurs seeking to raise money invariably began the process by contacting prospective investors and then following up with copies of their business plans. Today, entrepreneurs increasingly begin the process by launching their ventures in some form, and then conducting formal presentations to explain their vision. Here is a summary comparison of the approaches:

Approaches to Investment

Old Approach	*New Approach*
(Pre-1995)	*(Post Internet Revolution)*
Send business plan (BP)	Get business going (bootstrap) to potential investors
Await response	Present to potential investors
Keep re-working BP	Write synopsis letter
Seek enough for 2-4 yrs	Always in financing mode

Pack it in if don't raise $$ in 3-4 months	Show staying power
Lie low 'til all ducks lined up	Get publicity early on
Raise money and forget BP	In regular contact with likely investors
Seek sales after raise $$	Show real sales early on
Work out business model after raise $$	Demo a workable business model
Show sales	Complete BP

As you can see, the business plan hasn't disappeared from the landscape, but rather has assumed a much different role in the process of financing and building a business. Instead of being tackled at the start of the business development process, it is left to later stages, after more critical tasks have been dealt with and the business is up and running in some form. This new role for the business plan reflects the fact that professional investors will no longer assume technology and other significant risk; they demand sales or similar customer confirmation before committing.

So if you are focusing your startup efforts primarily on following the conventional wisdom and investing 100 or more hours in writing a business plan in the expectation it will help you raise investment funds, you may be making a big mistake. You may be better off disposing of your business plan, and pursuing a totally different approach. The goal of *Burn Your Business Plan!* is to help you shake off the old approach—which is still preached in many books and taught at many business schools—and make the transition to the new approach, which will save you time and money, and enable you to reach your business goals sooner than otherwise. It is a transition from reliance on a written business plan to other forms of planning—and doing.

This book is based on my many years of experience working with entrepreneurs, as well as the input of 42 venture capitalists who were surveyed about their approaches to evaluating and investing in growing companies. While I recognize that most entrepreneurs raise investment funds from "informal investors"—family and friends—I sought out the views of venture capitalists because they are indicative of the investor mindset, while having the advantages of being more readily identifiable and accessible. Moreover, venture capitalists tend to apply more formal evaluation methods than "angels" and other informal investors, so if venture capitalists are reducing emphasis on business plans, then it's a safe bet all investors are doing so.

Burn Your Business Plan! guides you in three separate sections that:

1. Demonstrate why the old approach is no longer viable;
2. Describe the tools of the new approach;
3. Lead you through the process of obtaining financing.

The techniques described in this book are relevant whether or not you plan to obtain investment funds. To achieve the fullest potential of your business, you always need to be actively improving your investor relations, regardless of the exact nature of your investors and your relationships. ■

Part I

New Perspectives on Business Planning

For much of the Post-World-War-II economic boom, business planning has been equated with writing a 30-to-40-page document neatly organized into such topics as "Strategy," "Marketing" "Production," and "Finances." That document was accepted as the ticket of admission for entrepreneurs trying to raise investment funds.

For any number of reasons, which are discussed in the first part of this book, that is no longer the case. Breaking old habits and establishing new approaches is challenging in all areas of business, and life. Because entrepreneurs have been so heavily browbeaten to write business plans, I believe it is essential to explain in some detail the problems with the conventional approach. This section of the book examines why the conventional written business plan has become incompatible with important trends in the business and economic environment. It makes its case by examining actual business plans, research on business planning, and the experiences of successful entrepreneurs.

Once the dangers of the old approach are clear, the reasons for adopting the new approach hopefully become more compelling. Sections II and III then provide an alternative approach to communicating with investors, obtaining funds, and building your business.

Chapter 1

Raising Money in an Age of High Anxiety
Why Investors Have Business Plan Phobia

CHAPTER SUMMARY

Investors are increasingly unsettled by all the economic, political, and other uncertainties that are now part of our lives. As a result, investors want ever more reassurance from entrepreneurs before handing out investment funds. A written business plan is no longer enough. Indeed, it has slipped in its importance to investors. They look first and foremost for tangible business success.

"If your business proposition is misguided, no amount of business plan technique will help your cause."

—Venture capitalist participant in survey for this book

I f you're an entrepreneur seeking investment funds for a new business, here's a typical scenario: You inquire with a venture capitalist or "angel" (private investor) you've been referred to, and are told, "Send along a business plan. We'll let you know if we're interested."

What do you do? If you're like many entrepreneurs, you scour the Internet or buy a book for information on how to prepare a business plan, and rush headlong into a process that will ultimately consume 100 tedious hours or more to produce a 30-to-40-page written document. Eagerly, you send it along, and wait.

More than likely, you won't even hear back from the investor and, if you do, you'll receive a negative response— the investor isn't investing in your kind of business or isn't investing at all or you're seeking too much, or too little, in funding. The excuses go on and on as you send the business plan to prospective investor after prospective investor. As the weeks drag on, your business plan is becoming more and more out of date.

What's the problem here? Just because a prospective investor asks for a business plan doesn't mean that he or she really wants it. Nor does it mean that you have to send it.

Consider the response that many of us have when charities call us at home seeking contributions. "Send some information along and I'll consider it," you say. Then, when the information comes along, you quickly dispose of it.

Sometimes entrepreneurs forget that professional investors are people, too. And as people, what they say they want and what they really do want are often two different things. As economic, political, and other uncertainties have piled up around them, investors are increasingly demanding more tangible kinds of reassurance than a sheaf of papers containing rosy market, product, and financial projections can provide. Only they won't necessarily tell you that in so many words.

The Real World

Cheryl Marshall, a principal of Axxon Capital, a Boston-based venture capital firm that specializes in investing in businesses owned by women and minority entrepreneurs, speaks frequently to groups of entrepreneurs about obtaining financing. She invariably refers to the business plan as something that is important, advising entrepreneurs to explain in their plans such matters as "the real strategy."

But get her in private, as I did following a speech she gave to a group of early-stage entrepreneurs in mid-2001, and she communicates an entirely different viewpoint. "I don't read business plans," she told me. "I look at the entrepreneur." To back up her point, she said that of six investments her venture firm had made to that point, all the entrepreneurs had come to her via referrals from trusted sources rather than via business plans that had been sent to her. Business plans weren't part of what she wanted to examine. It wasn't that she was being dishonest in her speech to the entrepreneurs, it's just that, like so many professional investors, she tends to advise preparing a business plan as more of a knee-jerk reaction than anything else.

While most investors aren't as candid as Cheryl—for public consumption, at least—get them alone and in conversation, and many will tell you the same thing. Their exact words may be different—they don't take business plans very seriously, they don't get a lot of useful information out of business plans, they are too busy to read through all of them—but the bottom-line message is the same: The business plan as it is conceived and used by many entrepreneurs is passé. It has been corrupted to the point that it is over-emphasized by entrepreneurs, and under-utilized by investors.

This isn't to say that entrepreneurs should discontinue writing business plans, and that investors don't care at all about written plans. But in recent years, an important perception gap has grown between what entrepreneurs are worrying about, and spending time on, and what investors really care about, and consider in their investment decisions. Entrepreneurs have increasingly made the business plan an end in itself, and all the while investors have increasingly come to view the business plan as merely one part of a much larger process, and an ever-less-important one at that.

It is in their actions that investors make their real feelings known. Consider this tally assembled by Michael Gonnerman, a Boston-area financial adviser to growing technology companies and to angel investors. Of eight companies he has been involved with as an adviser and that raised investment funds or were acquired between 1999 and 2002, only one completed the investment/acquisition by virtue of having a complete written business plan. The other seven (one of which was a company I co-founded) succeeded via effective presentations, impressive sales, networking, and

13

sheer grit and determination. One of those seven (not my company) started out with a written plan, and discarded it early in its fundraising process, determining that the document was more a hindrance than a help in the effort.

Venture capitalists are increasingly waiving their business plan requirements. In my survey of 42 venture capitalists, 43% said they had invested in one or more businesses within the previous three years "without the benefit of having reviewed a complete business plan" of 15 to 40 pages. (For full results of the survey, see Appendix I.) This was unheard of in the pre-Internet-boom days. It's safe to say that a significant percentage of the remainder only reviewed a business plan very late in the investment process—at the investors' request as a part of their "due diligence" to closing a financing—so they could have something in their files in case backers questioned them later on.

One private investor told me that he has come to view business plans as the equivalent of "intellectual pushups." Nice exercise, but not necessarily relevant to anything in the real world.

The Underlying Issues

For entrepreneurs, there are really five sorts of problems here:

1. We're in a new age of anxiety and uncertainty.

Buddhist philosophers have long warned us about the dangers associated with seeking permanence in a world where everything is fundamentally impermanent. You don't have to be an expert in Buddhist philosophy to realize that America changed its perspective virtually overnight beginning September 11, 2001 when we were caught totally off-guard by a cataclysmic terrorist attack. The nation, and indeed the whole world, came face to face with the notion that impermanence and uncertainty are a more integral part of our lives than we had fully understood. That revelation created a great deal of anxiety among the population at large, and among investors in particular. A written business plan suggests an ability to look into the future with a reasonable degree of certainty. Handing a written business plan painting an upbeat three-year scenario to a person skeptical about what is going to happen in the next hour, day, or week doesn't make as much sense as it once did.

2. The business of business has changed.

The events of September 11, 2001 merely put an exclamation point to the truism that business is moving and changing more quickly than ever before. Business experts have written reams about how quickly business is changing, driven in large measure by the Internet and related instant communication, but few have made any connection between this development and the business plan.

One recent book that begins to explain the process is *Collaborative Communities: Partnering for Profit in the Networked Economy* by Jeffrey Shuman and Janice Twombly. It focuses on the increasing importance of timing—"the ability to move at exactly the right strategic moment"—in determining business success, and notes, "In the absence of understanding how to tell when it's time to take a step, many people have resorted to using arbitrary measures of time. For example, they prepare three-year to five-year business plans, 12-month budgets, conduct quarterly reviews, and the like. The difficulty is that timing cannot be preplanned."

Jeffry Timmons, a Babson College professor and one of the deans of entrepreneurship in the U.S., made this observation in a new-course document, "Historically, from semiconductors and mini-computers, to PCs, cellular and the Internet, ... early 'bird-dog' bets by U.S. venture capitalists are precursors of new technologies and industries to come. Up until now, an industry's take-off has typically taken 15-20 years *after* the initial venture capital investments. In today's Web and IT world the… revolution is likely to happen in half that time."

3. Investor approaches have changed.

Business plans were originally conceived idealistically, in the Post-World-War II venture capital world that evolved, as something every entrepreneur should do. After all, everyone should plan, right? But entrepreneurs never took this "planning thing" seriously. They knew that the real purpose of a business plan was to obtain investment funds. So if writing a business plan was something that all these crazy investors really wanted, the entrepreneurs would fill the market demand.

The only problem is that the business plan routine is increasingly out of synch with how investors go about their business. Business plans are no longer what many investors necessarily examine first when evaluating a company. Over the last decade, while the business plan mantra has spread far and wide, other means of communicating with investors have sprung up. These include Web sites, PowerPoint presentations, online media, and trade shows. Venture capitalists and other private investors spend most of their time seeking out the next big thing, not waiting to review the business plans that pile up on their desks.

Because professional investors are sometimes in competition with other professional investors to get to the most promising companies first, the investors don't necessarily communicate their approaches to entrepreneurs. Instead, the investors often automatically tell entrepreneurs to "send your business plan along." All the while, the investors spend lots of time hunting for businesses that meet pre-determined criteria that are most important to them. Thus, if they've targeted restaurant chains, they spend time hanging out at restaurant industry conferences and courting entrepreneurs with success in the field. They network with bankers, accountants, and lawyers for leads on especially interesting businesses.

In other words, they're searching for the most compelling, attractive, interesting situations possible. The key word is "searching," as opposed to waiting. They want to find these situations, or at least feel they've found them.

When entrepreneurs do the searching and locate investors via the Internet or some source book, investors are suspicious, and back off. They delegate to interns and administrative assistants the chore of reviewing business plans that come in over the transom, much like book editors delegate to the most junior editors the chore of reviewing book manuscripts that come in over the transom.

As time has gone on, and professional investors have become ever more inundated with business plans, the investors have become ever less likely to read the plans. And they're looking at other things besides the business plan to make their investment decisions.

4. Jittery investors need more convincing than ever to part with funds.

For all their high-sounding talks about business models, return on equity, and growth curves, professional private investors are heavily influenced by emotional factors. They want to invest when the economy is strong and stock markets are setting new highs each week, and to back off when the opposite is true. During 2001 and 2002, for example, the latter was true.

What that means for entrepreneurs is that they have to go further than they might ever have thought possible to raise the money they need. That means waiting longer, persuading more, and keeping the business going without financing—until financial backers are finally persuaded by your persistence and staying power to provide backing.

5. The venture creation process has changed radically.

Perhaps most important, the actual process whereby the most successful new companies are created appears to be changing before our eyes. Venture creation is now a much more familiar activity to an ever-wider segment of the population, as increasing numbers of women have begun enterprises and more people of all types have worked in startup and early-stage businesses. Increasingly, individuals test the waters of prospective new businesses by selling items on Ebay or elsewhere on the Internet, or on a part-time basis. All this isn't to say that starting a business is a casual affair for many people, but more individuals appear willing to take the plunge and hang out a shingle.

Corrupted Process

Despite all the changes in the business world just described, one thing has remained unchanged: the belief by entrepreneurs and those who advise them in the importance of written business plans. In the world of business and investing, there's usually a problem when everyone begins doing the same thing. When too many toy makers turn out mini-scooters, you have an over supply, prices plummet, and no one is making money. When too many investors are buying stocks, as they were during the late 1990s, it's usually the prelude to a big fall. So it is with business plans.

Today's startup entrepreneurs have been browbeaten with the same mantra: Before you do anything else, you must write a business plan. There's some evidence, which I discuss later in this book, that as many as half of today's startup entrepreneurs are preparing business plans—a much higher percentage than for established businesses. There's also evidence, which I discuss later, that writing all those plans may actually be counterproductive to the companies' business prospects.

Just to compound the problem of quantity, there's a problem of quality as well. Among other things:

They all seem to look the same. For this we can thank the many business plan software programs, templates, and "libraries" of business plans. The problem is that while investors want businesses run by stars who perform

18

spectacularly, these "tools" suggest a sameness that makes it difficult for investors to pick out the jewels. Many business plans are thus being produced in almost mass production form via software and templates that don't allow for the reflection and creative thinking that must be embodied in a business. It's comparable to food processing that inadvertently eliminates or destroys key ingredients from food.

They all seem to sound the same. Probably that's because they so often use the same grandiose Forrester and Gartner Group marketing studies and Excel spreadsheet projections showing sales tripling and quadrupling each year. In my survey of 42 venture capitalists, 90% said that to only a modest or poor extent do the business plans they see "provide a clear and accurate assessment of the company's current operations and likely prospects for the future"; only 10% said the business plans they review do the job to a great extent.

They have little relation to reality. That's because there is no business reality without an operating business. When entrepreneurs spend most of their time writing a business plan, they have less time to do the hard work necessary to actually build the business. The resulting plans are empty promises, just like many of the advertisements we see on television and hear on the radio each day.

No one uses them to run their businesses. It's practically a given among entrepreneurs and venture capitalists that once a business receives investment funding, the business plan gets put on a shelf, never to be heard from again. In other words, the business plan has been used to raise money, not to plan the business.

Some Examples

To give emphasis to the previous section, I have excerpted segments of plans from among 40 judged to be the best in a recent major business plan contest sponsored by a private events promoter and held on the campus of a major university. I haven't identified the sponsor, businesses, or entrepreneurs, and in some cases have changed names or industries so they can't be identified. But the language of each plan is preserved.

It's important to remember in reviewing these that they are just a very few of the total number of plans that inundate investors. No one knows exactly how many plans are written, and I'm not sure it's worth anyone's while to do a survey to find out. But it has to be a huge number. Consider this, from a 2001 study of entrepreneurship worldwide by the Kauffman Center for Entrepreneurial Leadership and Babson College: An estimated 150 million people out of 1.6 billion in 29 countries studied (including the U.S., Japan, Mexico, and France) are "creating or growing new businesses."

Now surely most of these individuals won't be preparing business plans, but if just 10% did, that's 15 million business plans being produced each year. Actually, the number could be much higher. A research project to investigate the impact of business planning undertaken by three University of Illinois business professors—G.T. Lumpkin, Rodney C. Shrader, and Gerald E. Hills—and presented at the annual Babson College Entrepreneurship Research Conference in 1998 (and discussed in detail in Chapter 3), found that half of the 54 startup businesses surveyed had prepared written business plans; this was a much higher percentage than for more established businesses. Whatever the actual number, lots of plans are being turned out each year.

The nub of the problem confronting many entrepreneurs is that they focus so early and fully on writing a business plan that they don't have all that much to report and assess in terms of what they've accomplished. As a result, they devote their plans to discussing what they expect will happen. In their attempts to build up interest in something that in reality is far from completion, the entrepreneurs often let their imaginations run wild. Thus, their plans are prone to all sorts of problems, including the following:

Hype: When the imagination takes over, the end result tends to be hype. Entrepreneurs in highly competitive markets string together a few marketing projections and hopes, pop in a few exclamation points, and, presto, they have a huge opportunity that they are poised to dominate. Two-thirds of the venture capitalists in my survey cited "too much… hype" as a "significant shortcoming" in the plans they see. For example:

> *SpecialGaming seeks to capture the largest share of the burgeoning one billion dollar gross revenue online gaming market! We will create the first Internet Web site dedicated to Internet tournament play for cash! Our most significant advantage is ownership of the only comprehensive collection of "dot com Tournament" names from the following categories—board games, card games, casino games, puzzles, trivia, and sports. This key advantage will make our business easy to remember without having to rely on a "burn cash" strategy for continued brand recognition.*

Overly ambitious business models: The advent of the Internet and its futuristic technological implications seems to have encouraged many entrepreneurs to describe such complex entities that it's difficult to determine what the company's business will be. Here's an example, from a company in India:

Business Model: Action will set up 15 centers all over India for carrying out its activities. The cities selected are major towns having population in range of 2-10 million. The center at Indore is already in operation and shortly Delhi and Mumbai centers are starting. The major activities are IT-Education, IT-Enabled Services and Software.

In my survey of venture capitalists, "insufficient explanation of the business model" was cited as a serious problem in business plans by just over half the respondents. The business model refers to how a company structures its marketing approach to serve customers, and make money. Too often, there's an unclear notion of how the customer will benefit from the company's product or service.

Lingo: One of the main reasons investors tune out on business plans is because they contain lots of lingo—technical mumbo jumbo that is either difficult to non-techies to understand or else so overused it has lost its meaning. A classic example of the latter is the term "solution." Everyone, it seems, is producing a "solution" to some problem.

This is a problem similar to the previous one of not being able to understand a company's business. Put enough lingo in, and you can't be sure what a company does. Two-thirds of my venture capital respondents cited lingo overload as a significant problem in the business plans they review. Consider these business plan opening statements:

Business Model: Specialized Production Management information technology solution for the $30 billion-a-year filmed entertainment industry. Build a vertical portal for the global, fragmented elements that comprise this high-profile, niche vertical market.

෴

BDE provides a collaborative software platform for business technology management (BTM). This software platform solves the traditional disconnect between business and technology professionals by providing a single, automated environment that simplifies and aligns decision-making. It comprises a suite of modeling applications, a profile-driven knowledgebase of codified business and technology information, and a vendor collaboration interchange for solution providers and user organizations. The users of this platform include a cross-functional team of business and technology representatives, while the beneficiaries are members of the corporate leadership team.

Crazy projections: Entrepreneurs know that professional investors like to latch onto fast-growing companies in fast-growing markets. What they may not fully appreciate is that "financial projections too far removed from reality (either optimistic or pessimistic)," is the most significant shortcoming venture capitalists identify in the business plans they see—by more than 80% of the respondents in my survey.

Connecting a young company to a fast-growing market is much more than a matter of words, such as in this plan:

The restaurant pager market is a new market growing rapidly. 2.5% of all eating establishments or 20,500 restaurant locations are potential customers. The market in 2001 was $300 million with a long term growth rate of 10% to 15% per year. In three years, ABC Paging plans to acquire 15% of the market or 3,000 restaurant locations to give us $20 million in revenues.

23

Inappropriate management team information:
Most entrepreneurs know how closely investors examine the
people involved in launching a young company. But how
you go about communicating that you have top people is
another matter. Here is an example of how not to
communicate that you have the best people:

> *DEF's expert team is comprised of industry leaders
> and professionals that account for over 100 years of
> top management experience in the entertainment,
> media, telecommunications and technology
> industries, and well over 250 years of management
> experience within its technology development team.*

They sound more like they should be in an old-age
home than starting a new business. It's nice to have many
years of experience, but investors also want to know how the
entrepreneurs performed during all those earlier years on the
job. Did their companies grow significantly? Were they
acquired? Failure to elaborate suggests that the outcome was
negative.

The Messages

Aside from the fact that there are too many questionable
plans being churned out, what other messages should you
glean from the preceding? For the purposes of your own
fundraising efforts, I'd point to three:

1. The business plan shouldn't be the first thing you
do. I discuss in Section II of this book seven steps that
should precede a business plan, and are likely to be more
effective than a business plan in helping you raise money.
2. When you begin preparing a plan, don't just review
other plans to determine how your plan should read. There
are so many bad plans out there that you risk falling into the
old garbage-in-garbage-out syndrome.

3. The key messages you want to communicate to prospective investors have to do with what you have accomplished or are about to accomplish, not your dreams for the future.

Costly Implications

There's a rule in business that goes something like this: The younger your business, the fewer mistakes it can afford.

What this rule suggests is that the smaller your business, the fewer resources it can afford to waste. Conversely, the bigger your business, the more mistakes you get. Thus, AT&T could bungle for years and years, and still stay in business. But even AT&T may be running out of bungling chances.

Here's the disconnect for entrepreneurs: They worry about writing plans when all investors care about is the business—whether entrepreneurs truly understand their markets, can grow quickly, be profitable, and have the leadership skills to negotiate all the many bumps in the road. Instead of spending their time writing plans, entrepreneurs need to do all these other things. ■

Chapter 2

Ask the Wrong Question and You'll Get the Wrong Answer--
Where We've Gone Wrong in Thinking About Business Plans

CHAPTER SUMMARY

Even though written business plans are no longer a top priority for many investors, there are lots of folks who'd just as soon not notice. The writing of the business plan has become a lucrative industry for business writers, book and magazine publishers, and academics who teach courses on writing business plans. Any change in the status quo threatens their interests. Here is what is wrong with the business plan contests and other hype that encourage an undue focus on writing business plans, and how to put the hype into its proper perspective.

"Many business plans do a decent job of pointing at potential opportunities, but they aren't very compelling as to why I should back this management team in going after that opportunity."

—Venture capitalist participant in survey for this book

On an Inc.com discussion forum in mid-2001, an entrepreneur, James, posted this question: "I have an idea to start a business, but I can't write a business plan by myself. So my question is, how much does it cost to have someone, such as a consulting company, write a business plan for me?"

The half dozen or so executives who responded to James each tried to be helpful. One suggested that he should expect to pay $75 per hour, or a $5,000 flat fee to get a credible consultant. Another said a range of $3,000 to $8,000 should be about right, and "if you can find someone who charges much less than $3,000, they're probably not

27

going to be professionals." A third agreed with the previous two, saying $3,000 to $10,000 is the right range.

Three other respondents tried to steer James toward getting free help from university-based Small Business Development Centers (SBDCs), or else from a group of business school students supervised by a professor.

No one thought to question the wisdom of James' intention of bringing in consultants to help him write a business plan. Was it appropriate for him to be thinking about spending as much as $10,000 to write a business plan for a startup company? Even if he could get the job done for free from an SBDC, should he be devoting possibly 40, 50, or 100 hours to collaborating on the plan? Is it possible he should be devoting his time and scarce capital to other tasks that might be more productive to his fledgling business? What were the odds that the plan would actually lead to financing?

The executives who responded to James' question weren't providing unreasonable answers to the question being asked. But the question being asked was reflective of how entrepreneurs automatically assume that writing a business plan, or getting it written for them, is a high-priority task.

What's wrong with entrepreneurs in search of capital automatically assuming they need to invest huge sums of time and/or money in writing a business plan? The entrepreneurs may be asking the wrong question, taking the wrong action—and wasting precious resources.

As I explained in the first chapter, entrepreneurs are turning out too many business plans that venture capitalists and other professional investors aren't reading. Yet entrepreneurs continue turning out business plans as one of their first orders of business. Why do they continue to write plans?

If It Seems too Good to be True...

In our society, we love "magic" solutions to our problems. Hundreds of diet books and plans—each seemingly with its own special "guaranteed" approach—come out each year, leading many people to embark on weight-loss programs. In similar fashion, business plans have become a seemingly magical solution for entrepreneurs trying to figure out an easy way to obtain money from investors—you write a plan, show it to investors, and they write you a check. It was never that simple, of course, but during the mid and late 1990s, it often seemed that way. And certainly there were enough stories about that order of events that many entrepreneurs believed the scenario to be true.

The problem with any such magic solution is that even if it was true, the magic doesn't last forever. Most people who shed pounds in the first few weeks of a diet soon find the weight coming back. Indeed, the problem of obesity seems to be getting worse, in the U.S. and in other developed countries.

Even magic solutions that seem foolproof for long periods of time can fizzle out. Thus, antibiotics seemed for much of the twentieth century to be miracle drugs. They became so over-used, though, that bacteria increasingly have become immune to the effects of antibiotics, and there are now some bacterial infections that can't be treated with antibiotics.

There's an analogy between antibiotics and business plans. Antibiotics have become over-used in part because neither the medical profession nor consumers were willing to consider other approaches for fighting disease—for example, using diet, exercise, and meditative techniques to build up their immune systems and thus reduce bacterial infections, and the need for antibiotics. Or simply holding back before prescribing antibiotics, so they wouldn't be prescribed for viral infections, and other inappropriate situations.

Business plans similarly have become over-used, a crutch of sorts, by entrepreneurs who have been encouraged to seek out a simple and straightforward approach to raising money for their ventures. The entrepreneurs would rather not think about other ways to deal with the investor challenge—more creative ways to communicate the attractiveness of the business opportunity to an audience that is increasingly cynical about the plans being churned out in such vast quantities.

The reason such seemingly magical solutions develop is that they are one-dimensional. A single solution to a complex problem almost invariably loses its luster over time as the outside world changes in ways that the single solution doesn't account for. Our public school system and its regimented approach to learning have fallen into disfavor, for example, because of rigidity, and only in recent years has it begun to change.

So Why Do We Keep Doing Business Plans?

The difficulty associated with contradicting an established practice like business planning is that there is an entrenched "establishment" that has a stake in continuing a process that is beneficial (read "makes money"). Consider the scope of the business planning "industry

Book publishers. There are now hundreds of books having to do with preparing a business plan. A search on Amazon.com under "business plan" yields more than 500 books on the subject; there were perhaps a dozen or so in the early 1990s. These books yield ongoing revenues to their publishers and authors (which I have shared in from my previous two books).

Magazine publishers. The subject of business plans is "an evergreen" for both print and online business magazines catering to entrepreneurs. Publications like *Entrepreneur, Inc.,* and *Fortune Small Business* promote the idea of business planning with how-to articles on the subject and reinforcing statements about the necessity of a business plan. A search on Inc.com for "business plan" turns up nearly 2,000 articles and related documents (including chapters from my books).

College and university courses. There are now hundreds of courses at colleges and business schools devoted to writing a business plan. A decade ago, there were only a handful. Undergraduate and MBA students spend many hours writing plans for businesses they are either thinking about starting, or are in the process of starting. In a course, the students assess each other's plans and submit them to professors for feedback. These courses yield important tuitions to the colleges.

Software companies. Software makers of all types have come up with fill-in-the-blank business plan templates. Some of these are stand-alone programs you purchase, while others operate online. Either way, you typically answer questions about your industry, marketing strategy, sales projections, and other items, and the software spits out a completely formatted plan.

Assorted promoters and consultants. Hundreds of consultants seek to fill in the gaps that the books, courses, and software programs miss. The consultants will do everything from evaluate business plans (I came across one on the Internet that charges $290 for an evaluation of up to 20 pages) to actually write them, sometimes charging in excess of $10,000 for the effort.

Business plan contests. In addition, there are dozens of business plan contests that fan the flames even more. Colleges and universities from around the country, along with consulting firms, newspapers, and other organizations now sponsor contests that purport to select the best business plans from a group of students or other entrants. Harvard Business School, for example, offers prizes of $20,000 in cash and professional services to each of two winners.

Why We Do It

The reason for all this activity is that business planning sells. I don't know this industry's annual revenues, but I would suspect they're pretty significant, certainly many millions of dollars.

But perhaps more important, the business plan is highly specific and predictable. It's a straightforward task for a facile writer or consultant to take all the business plan books that have previously been written and adapt the same material into a new book. It's not especially complicated for a professor to develop a course outline about business plans, and just teach the same thing year after year. It's straightforward for a programmer to build software that spits out a plan. And business plan contests with prize money to the winners? What a seemingly constructive way of attracting attention to the sponsor, and creating a little competition in the process.

What makes the business plan attractive to all these "sellers" is that prospective entrepreneurs, the "buyers," view the business plan as a required document to even approach prospective investors. Moreover, the task of preparing a business plan is daunting to entrepreneurs.

This leads to an intriguing marketplace situation. The sellers have something that is easy to produce, and a huge waiting market that perceives the product as absolutely essential and difficult to produce.

This was all fine so long as the product was absolutely essential. But once it is no longer so important, what are the producers to do? Well, if you are a maker of buggy whips in the early twentieth century or a producer of printed encyclopedias in the late twentieth century, you better find something else to make, because the market will surely abandon you and run to the more modern substitute.

But if you aren't inclined to change, you may just try to continue promoting your idea, and hope that the marketplace doesn't notice how much things have changed. And that is what the business plan industry has done—fan the flames about the importance of the business plan, even as the realities of the marketplace are changing dramatically.

Even some of the most active promoters are beginning to have second thoughts about much of this hype. Consider the reflections of Steven Robbins, founder of VentureCoach.com, on his stint as a judge at the Harvard Business School and Brown University business plan contests (posted on his Web site, www.venturecoach.com):

> *The team which had their business up and running and was proving it profitable did not win their semifinal round. Maybe because their business was not sexy and high tech?*
>
> *The judging criteria contained implicit value judgments about "good" businesses. High growth, huge market cap, original ideas were given a premium. In fact, my personal favorite plan in each competition was for a limited-growth opportunity. In the Brown competition, it was a limited opportunity with a me-too product!...*
>
> *...The judging criteria sometimes judged qualities of the idea, not whether the plan handled those qualities. For example, a criterion was "originality of the idea." Originality is fun, but it isn't necessarily a good criterion for a business plan competition. How about: "do the entrepreneurs recognize how original their idea is[n't] and have they taken steps to get the most out of the opportunity, given their degree of originality?" Sometimes originality is detrimental! Me-too products have produced spectacular market successes (can you say, "Windows?" "Blockbuster?" "General Motors?").*

My actual rankings reflected my feelings about the team, as expressed through their writing. The well-thought-out, clear, concise plan left me with the thought that even if the idea didn't work as expected, the entrepreneurs would find a way to make things work. Other plans had good product ideas, but wildly unrealistic marketing-speak plans left me afraid that their business judgment would be more influenced by Business 2.0 *buzzwords than by their ability to respond to the real world.*

Having served for several years as a judge at one college's business plan contest, I have had similar misgivings. I've found it difficult to pass qualitative judgment about businesses that exist only as ideas on 30 pages of paper. So I've fallen into the trap of looking for glitz. Who does the best job of snowing readers about a potentially huge opportunity? Yet I've gone along with such judging. After all, "The show must go on."

What's the Problem?

If you accept my previous argument that entrepreneurs are spending too much time preparing business plans that won't influence investors' decisions, then it seems apparent that the business plan industry is leading entrepreneurs astray. Too often, you are obsessing about preparing a business plan when you should be out doing the grunt work that is part and parcel of starting a business.

What exactly am I talking about? I'm talking about an industry that in the process of marketing its products is leading entrepreneurs astray, has lost sight of the reality of business, and is creating a number of myths about the business plan. Here are some of those myths:

1. *It's a ticket of admission.* The book publishers especially love to promote the sense of

34

insecurity—that if you don't do a business plan right off the bat, you won't be taken seriously by investors. The implication: Not only won't you get your money, but you'll be embarrassed in the process.

2. *It's easy.* The software publishers are fond of this notion. Just fill in the blanks and, presto, you'll have a business plan. Of course, as we all know, if something is too easy, there's probably a problem with it. So it is with business plan preparation. If you prepare a plan like everyone else's you'll probably come out like most everyone else—with no investment funds.

3. *It's a necessary exercise.* The colleges and universities in their role as knowledge advocates push this one, emphasizing the thought process behind preparing a business plan that is something inherently beneficial. There is no question that the exercise of assembling a business plan is useful for some entrepreneurs and business students under the guidance of experienced professors. But there's also evidence that the planning process, in this day and age of extremely rapid change, may actually be counterproductive. That evidence is the subject of the next chapter.

Chapter 3

Is Planning a Useful Exercise?
What the Research Shows

CHAPTER SUMMARY
Any number of celebrity entrepreneurs have succeeded without written plans.
Nor did they start their enterprises with a search for investors. And it's not just
celebrities who have done very well without written plans. A critical examination
of extensive academic research on business planning suggests that focusing
heavily on planning can actually be counter-productive. Here are six reasons why
business plans may be hazardous to your future wealth.

*"The process of business planning should focus more on testing and refining
your thinking about the business model and strategy and less on writing."*
—Venture capitalist participant in survey for this book

I f there's anything that resonates in our society, it's
celebrities. Oprah tells us what books to read,
Martha Stewart tells us how to entertain (though not how to
invest), and Tiger Woods tells us how to golf.

It's the same thing for entrepreneurs. When it comes time
to prepare a business plan, entrepreneurs want to see what
the celebrities did.

I've been a promoter of that approach myself. One of my
books on business planning, *How to Really Create a
Successful Business Plan*, has been marketed heavily based
on the fact that it contained excerpts of "celebrity" business
plans, from the founders of Pizza Hut, Ben & Jerry's, and
Celestial Seasonings.

When you read the biographies of Bill Gates, Michael
Dell, and Steve Case, you find all kinds of examples of their
perseverance, passion, smarts, risk taking, and other such
qualities that help companies succeed.

Gates dropped out of Harvard University after his freshman year to develop a programming language, which eventually led to development of DOS and the launch of the enterprise that turned into Microsoft.

Michael Dell sold mail order computers out of his dorm room at the University of Texas in Austin in an enterprise that revolutionized the selling of computers and became Dell Computer.

Steve Case in the late 1980s became a marketing consultant to a tiny computer game company and online service, and eventually transformed it into what we came to know as America Online, or AOL.

In reading the stories of these entrepreneurs, you never see anything like, "And then he prepared a business plan."

Certainly they prepared business plans of some kinds at various points in the growth of their businesses, to satisfy investor requirements or make a presentation to a board of directors. But the point is that preparing a business plan wasn't central to their success.

Nor has preparing a business plan been key to other famous entrepreneurs. Anita Roddick didn't prepare a business plan when she launched and grew the world-wide retail chain, Body Shop, nor did Frank Carney when he launched Pizza Hut (though he began writing business plans years later when the company was large enough to go public) or Debbie Fields when she launched Mrs. Fields' Cookies.

What's the common theme in the stories of these entrepreneurs? It's certainly not the business plan. It's also not about outside financing. Rather, it's about doing the business. Creating and selling the product or service, with little or no money. Bootstrapping, as it's come to be known.

Yet we keep searching for some holy grail in their stories, some document or other pixie dust that will give us the magic solution. If we can't find it in celebrities, we look for it in just ordinary businesses. There's at least one Web site that offers small payments (about $50) to companies that allow it to stockpile their business plans so that other entrepreneurs can review the plans before writing their own.

Some Scary Implications

The previous anecdotal information suggests a number of potential implications about the business plan that you should consider:

- A business plan may not be as important as we have been led to believe in winning investor and other backing;
- Winning investor backing may not be as important as we think in launching a business;
- Studying the business plans of other entrepreneurs, even those in your own industry, as guidance for preparing your own may be counterproductive.

And there are two other potential implications that are much more significant than the ones I've just listed:

1. What if preparing a business plan isn't actually helpful to the eventual success of a business?

2. Or, even worse, what if a business plan is actually counter-productive to a company's prospects?

These last two potential implications are very threatening to the business plan industry because they hit at the fallback argument of all business-planning proponents: Even if writing a business plan doesn't help you win investment funds, you'll at least have reaped the many benefits of having gone through the planning process, and you'll have a written plan your company can use to help you succeed. As allbusiness.com, an online small business information site, put it in an article about common errors entrepreneurs make in business planning: "Of course, the biggest mistake of all is failing to create a business plan in the first place. Planning is hard work, and there's no guarantee it will make your business succeed. But a good plan is still the best way to turn your vision into a realistic, coherent business."

I assert that there are more effective ways than traditional business planning to invest your time and reap even greater benefits, as I detail in Section 2, immediately following.

Surprising Research Results

Interestingly, there's been a considerable amount of research done on the benefits of business planning. One of the most thorough studies was a research project undertaken by three University of Illinois business professors—G.T. Lumpkin, Rodney C. Shrader, and Gerald E. Hills-- and presented at the annual Babson College Entrepreneurship Research Conference in 1998.

This study examined business planning from two perspectives:

First, it conducted a "literature review," whereby it examined the dozen or so significant studies on business planning that had been conducted over the previous approximately 20 years.

Second, it studied the impact of planning on 94 companies—54 newly formed companies and 40 established firms.

These scholars were keenly aware of the importance of their study, when they observed:

"The importance of planning to performance is a central premise in the entrepreneurship and strategic management literature. The business plan is regarded by many as an essential element of a successful startup; ongoing planning efforts are considered vital to continued success...Conventional wisdom and anecdotal evidence appear to take it for granted that planning positively influences firm performance. Some scholars have concluded that lack of planning or poor planning may lead to firm failure. Furthermore, venture capitalists report that a majority of entrepreneurs could avoid failure through better analysis of external circumstances."

Yet in their literature review, these researchers found disturbing issues associated with formal business planning. Their analysis of previous studies found that "the planning-performance relationship is not as straightforward as conventional wisdom suggests. In fact, findings have been so contradictory that some scholars have called the planning-performance relationship tenuous, concluded that planning may not be necessary at all, or argued that planning may actually hinder firm performance." (I've omitted the references to the authors of the studies alluded to. You can find more of the study and a Web link in Appendix 2.)

The results of their own study of 94 companies were equally intriguing, and disturbing. Of the 54 newly formed companies, half had prepared a written business plan, while only 12 of the 40 established firms had written plans. The fact that a much higher percentage of startup firms had prepared business plans "may be a reflection of the current business startup climate in which banks, venture capitalists, the SBA (Small Business Administration), and teachers of entrepreneurship nearly all consistently promote the usefulness and necessity of developing a written business plan."

When it came to correlating the business planning to performance of the startup companies, the researchers found some surprises. Of five types of planning investigated (financial, competitive, market, etc.), four failed to show a positive correlation to company performance; only financial projections were positively related, and "competitive analysis was negatively related to financial strength. This finding is especially notable because, among established firms, competitive analysis was the only planning variable that contributed positively to performance." In other words, startup companies that planned didn't necessarily perform better than companies that didn't plan, and in the area of competitive analysis, actually did worse.

41

The researchers' conclusion? "There was no strong relationship between performance and the use of a formal business plan."

What's the Problem?

How is it that a practice that is almost in the "Mom and apple pie" category is possibly bad for your business health?

No one knows for sure because, as the University of Illinois researchers suggest, the research that has been done is so contradictory. Some of it finds value in planning while some of it suggests that planning is counter-productive. Here are some of the potential fallacies associated with business planning that I take from this research:

- *That you can capture the business startup process in a single written plan.* In fact, the process may be too dynamic and fast changing. You can capture a few ideas, perhaps, to help focus the management team. As the University of Illinois researchers observed, "…while planning and analysis are related to financial performance, this planning may not need to be in the form of a written business plan."
- *That formal business planning is a way to gain solidity in today's dynamic business environment.* The University of Illinois researchers pointed out that a number of researchers "suggest that flexibility is critical to the success of planning among young and small firms. Indeed, one of the most widely circulated criticisms of formal planning is that it yields too much rigidity. Proponents of this view maintain that plans channel attention and behavior to an unacceptable degree, driving out innovations that are not part of the plan…Taken as a whole, these arguments suggest that the performance of young and

small firms is more likely to be improved when those firms engage in informal planning and analysis."

- ***That writing a plan is a useful exercise for the founders.*** In fact, it can distract everyone from other more important tasks, like obtaining sales. And as the research suggests, the final written plan may have little or no influence on a company's performance.

- ***That the plan is a way to promote teamwork because it is something everyone can refer to.*** The process of working together to plan can encourage camaraderie. The main problem with this rationale is that once the plan is written, it tends to sit on shelves and desks gathering dust, and no one in the company ever looks at it again.

- ***That you need to capture the business' direction in a single written plan.*** The premise here is similar to the previous one—that somehow it is beneficial to be able to write key planning matters down and have them available in a single document. But if no one ever looks at the plan after it's completed, what's the purpose?

- ***That by imitating the business plan of a successful entrepreneur, some of that success will rub off on you.*** My feeling is that even if you could, you don't want to replicate someone else's business plan. You want your own business plan, reflecting the unique positioning and strategy of your business, not someone else's business. If you want to put it into writing, fine. But however you do your planning, it should reflect you and not someone else.

Learning from Celebrities

I don't mean to suggest in all this that celebrities have nothing to offer entrepreneurs. We can glean valuable business lessons from entrepreneurs who have been extraordinarily successful. The challenge is to take the right lessons rather than the wrong ones from their experiences. For example, no matter how much we study Bill Gates' approach to licensing and selling an operating system, or Steve Case's approach to growing an online service, the odds are heavily against another entrepreneur pulling off either of those feats.

I believe that it's a matter of picking and choosing very carefully. Here are some of the benefits I believe we can gain:

1. *We can become inspired.* Super successful entrepreneurs invariably had to be extraordinarily persistent, and many encountered near failure along the way. To the extent that such experiences help energize us, so much the better.

2. *We can come to appreciate the very special talents involved in developing a fast-growing business.* If you study the celebrity entrepreneurs, you will discover that they usually have some extraordinary talents. Michael Dell applied amazing organizational talents to conceive the kind of low-cost distribution approach he devised. Steve Case understood better than anyone the importance of making his online service easy to use, and in endlessly pushing consumers to try it.

3. *That the combination of people is often very important.* More often than not, the celebrity entrepreneurs don't do it alone—they have another person who provides key support. Anita Roddick, the creative genius behind the Body Shop retail chain, had her husband keeping her organized. Walt Disney had the creative genius to come up with his cartoon characters, but he also had his brother's managerial prowess to turn the creativity into a business.

Another way of looking at the celebrity factor is that we can learn about the requirements necessary to build a business rather than write a business plan. If we spend our time searching for a secret document setting it all down, we're dooming ourselves to a fruitless search that can only yield fool's gold. There are more effective ways to spend your time, which yield much greater benefits, and these techniques are the subject of Section 2, immediately following. ■

Part II

Seven Actions You Should Take *Before* Preparing a Business Plan

Now that I've trashed the notion of the business plan as a pillar of entrepreneurship, the natural follow-up question you might have is this: If I don't use a business plan to obtain investment funds, what do I use?

This section seeks to answer that question by viewing the process of obtaining investment funds through the twin lenses of effectiveness and resource allocation. You want to spend your limited time and money on the things that will get you the best results.

This section is comprised of seven steps that will likely serve you more effectively in raising money than a business plan. Some of the steps are conceptual in approach and others are highly specific and action oriented.

These steps really are recommended as approaches to explore *before* becoming engaged in writing a business plan, not *instead* of writing a business plan. By going through these steps, you will be better prepared to get your business off the ground and, should you need or desire to do so, to write a business plan.

Chapter 4

Look Inward: What Is Your Startup Karma?

CHAPTER SUMMARY

Investors typically focus first and foremost on the quality of a venture's personnel. This truism raises two key questions: Do you have the qualities to succeed in business and will potential investors recognize them? Your responses to five questions help reveal if you'll succeed or why you won't. As your business' most important asset, here are a few exercises to assess your startup karma.

"Convince me that you eat, sleep, and dream about all this."
—Venture capitalist participant in survey for this book

This is probably the most difficult chapter for me to write because it is the least tangible. It is the complete opposite of subsequent chapters, which advise you about the specifics of presentations, sales, public relations, and other such tasks. But it could well be the most important, because it is about getting inside yourself in ways to help you determine whether you are really ready to start or grow a business and whether you can connect with investors and customers in ways that will be essential if you are going to succeed.

Why is it so important to get inside yourself? After all, you may be thinking, I just want to grow this business and make a lot of money. I'll have plenty of time after I've made a ton of money to get inside myself.

It is exactly such thinking that helps explain why business plans are less believable than ever. Entrepreneurs are increasingly writing business plans that they think prospective investors want to read rather than writing plans that truly reflect what the business and the entrepreneurs behind it are all about.

Yet the one thing investors care most deeply about is the quality of the people running the businesses the investors back. In my survey of venture capitalists, this theme was cited again and again. Consider this result: When I asked the 42 venture capitalists to rate on a scale of one to ten the importance of eight items that they might use in evaluating a company as an investment opportunity (such as financial projections or expected market size), "the quality of the company's management team" received a ten-rating by 74% of respondents; by contrast, the two items that were closest were each given ten-ratings by only 26% of respondents.

For Love or Money?

Why is there a tendency for entrepreneurs to emphasize their plans rather than the commitment of the people behind the plans? In my view, the business plan industry, and in particular the colleges and business schools, must share in the blame. The professors are encouraging, and in some cases requiring, entrepreneurs to write plans about businesses they're just thinking about starting, so that they get the experience of writing a business plan. In the process, though, these instructors aren't emphasizing enough the self-examination that should be part of the business creation process.

As we saw in Chapter 1, too many entrepreneurs are writing business plans that have little connection with reality. That is because they are writing plans that they think investors want to read rather than business plans that capture the true essence of what the business is all about.

There are three basic problems with this approach, aside from the fact that it is a form of dishonesty, and dishonesty invariably creates all kinds of unforeseen issues.

1. *You won't fool investors.* Sure, many investors screwed up during the mid and late 1990s, funding companies that didn't

deserve to be funded. Investors are human and subject to the very human foibles of greed and poor judgment. But I think it's safe to say that investors have gotten over their carelessness and, if anything, are now more cautious than they were even before the dot-com debacle.

A study out of the United Kingdom in 1994, before the dot-com craze, illustrates this point. The research, from professors at the University of Southampton and the University of Ulster, examined 35 proposed deals presented to a group of informal investors, sometimes referred to as "angels." Approximately 70% were rejected in an initial review process that included examination of a business plan and, in some cases, meetings with the principals. More than one-fourth were rejected "after the syndicate had conducted its own detailed research on the marketplace and the principals," the study reported. The investment group was interested in investing in two of the proposals, but failed to conclude the negotiations successfully. None of the proposals had turned the investors on enough that they wrote a check.

In my survey of 42 venture capitalists, just over half said they invest in less than 1% of the deals that cross their desks; 96% invest in fewer than 5% of deals.

Most fundamentally, investors want to know what makes you tick. They understand that you and your team are the most important part of the equation, so they will search and probe as hard as they can to determine whether you "have what it takes" to succeed—whether you have the persistence, and can take the pressure of the inevitable difficulties that arise in any growing business.

2. *You won't fool the potential market.* Entrepreneurs often don't fully appreciate how difficult it is to actually sell products and services. That's because they haven't interacted in a meaningful way with prospective customers or clients. You need to be able to fully understand the market you are proposing to serve. In fact, I advocate in Chapter 10 that entrepreneurs have obtained significant positive feedback

from the marketplace before attempting to raise money so as to reduce the perceived market risk for investors.

3. *You will fool yourself.* The worst outcome is that you start a business you don't believe in, but you think will make money. We've all seen such businesses. The tired restaurant or retail store that the owner doesn't care about much any more. The gee-whiz high-tech business that the owners are desperately trying to sell because they aren't accomplishing what was expected. I've fallen into this trap myself, by taking on significant consulting assignments in exchange for equity (and thus effectively putting myself in the position of an entrepreneur) and then realizing that I took the assignment because I thought I could achieve a "quick hit." Quick hits are quite rare in the business world.

It's easy to say in such situations, "Well, I can sell the business. Or I can turn it over to others." But those steps are much much easier said than done.

I've often said that starting a business is a lot like marriage: It's much easier to get into than to get out of. You should always ask yourself this question: Is this business something I want to spend the next five to ten years of my life doing?

Karma and Your Business

The whole subject of looking inward is about more than not writing a business plan you don't fully believe in or making the right personal decisions. It's bigger than that. The best way of getting at it is to discuss it in terms of karma.

Karma in this context is different from the "good vibes" we generally think of it as. It has to do with your destiny, the total you. Here is how Sogyal Rinpoche explains it in his widely read book, *The Tibetan Book of Living and Dying*: "Karma…is best thought of as the infallible law of cause and effect that governs the universe…It means that whatever we do, with our body, speech, or mind, will have a corresponding result. Each action, even the smallest, is pregnant with its consequences."

Yes, it is that significant. Because the business you try to get support for is really you. It embodies not only your business and managerial expertise, but your personality, your spirit, your soul. That is why it must nearly always embody your commitment and passion if it is to have any chance of succeeding.

Questions to Ask Yourself

From a business viewpoint, you can begin to assess this whole matter of karma by asking yourself a number of basic questions:

Do you have the "right" personality? There's much debate about this issue among academics. Research suggests that certain types of personalities—those that are positive and persistent—are likeliest to succeed. Related to these attributes is leadership. Can you convince employees, suppliers, and yes, investors, to follow you into the great unknown that is a new and early-stage business?

Do you have the thinking skills? The key here is being able to see the big picture, and to avoid getting lost in the details. It's about the old saying, "He can't see the forest for the trees." As an entrepreneur, you need to be able to see the "forest" of the marketplace, the investor scene, and your own organization. The risk in not being able to see the larger view is that you'll get bogged down in the irrelevant and distracting details that cloud many business pictures.

Do you have the passion? You need to truly believe in what you're doing. Really care about what you are doing. If your passion is to help other people, then you must see that opportunity in your business. If your passion is to create beauty, then the product or service you sell must do that in a significant way to satisfy your internal drive.

Do you have all the skills you need? Key among the essential skills is an ability to delegate tasks. Too many entrepreneurs who are unable to move their companies past a certain level, such as $500,000 or $1 million annual sales, are those whom for whatever reasons aren't comfortable getting others to take on significant responsibility. They can't let go.

Can you handle serious pressure? No matter how well you scope out the market and finances, your business will endure difficult times. Key employees will leave at the worst possible time, customers will neglect to pay on time, and you'll fail to win some business you thought was a gimme. How well you pick up from such losses and move on will say a lot about your overall chances of succeeding, because there will be times you will be sorely tempted to pack it all in.

If you have all these attributes, you begin to have the karma that is so essential to successfully growing a business.

What Investors Really Want to Know

The reason you should ask yourself these questions early on, and continue to ask them as you actually begin your business, is that when you try to raise investment funds, the process will almost certainly be long and drawn out, even if a number of potential investors are interested in your business. Much of the reason it is drawn out is that investors tend to investigate carefully, and answer the questions posed in the previous section for themselves.

A significant part of what they are investigating is you, the entrepreneur. By investigating, I don't mean just doing reference and credit checks. They want to see first-hand how you perform under pressure. They want to see you make a presentation and answer their tough questions. They want to see how you handle the negotiations. They want to see how you behave when things look bleak.

An entrepreneur I know well, Laurel Touby, went through this process when she was trying to obtain financing for her company, mediabistro.com, a job board and community web site for publishing professionals. For three years prior to seeking investor backing, she had done everything any investor could ask for in terms of karma. She had launched the business as a free service based on her passionate interest in networking and helping freelancers obtain work. (She had spent many years both on-staff and as a freelancer, and so knew the highs and lows of the profession.) She had invested her own limited financial resources and time in establishing the business. And finally, she had proven the concept by virtue of the fact that media firms and publishers were paying to post help-wanted classifieds on her site, and revenues were growing sharply.

Finally, she decided that the business needed an infusion of capital to help it take off. When she approached a group of investors recommended by a business associate for the money, the group seemed very interested after she did a presentation, negotiated extensively, and finally wrote a business plan. But then they hesitated. They still weren't sure she had what it took to be a successful entrepreneur. To her, though, it seemed a stalling technique.

So Laurel sat down and wrote a passionate two-page letter explaining why she was the best qualified person to grow this business, and re-emphasizing how many milestones she had already achieved without any funding. She received her investment funds.

While the investors never exactly said so, it is clear that it was almost as if they were testing Laurel to see how hard she would push them. Rather than see her hard-hitting letter as overly pushy, they clearly saw it as an example of her fire and passion—two of the most important ingredients in making a business succeed.

The Entire Package

And if you have all of the sought after qualities, does the business you are proposing to create adequately reflect them all? This is about representing yourself and your business as they really are.

You communicate your karma in all kinds of ways. How you walk into a room. How your marketing brochures are put together. The appearance of your offices, and so forth.

If the entire package doesn't make sense, prospective investors will know. Two women entrepreneurs, Kelly O'Brien and Nancy Dailey, owners of a successful corporate consulting firm, discovered this first-hand in early 2000. They decided to abandon the stable consulting firm they had spent nine years building in favor of launching a potentially fast-growing online computer model to help women manage their money.

A *Wall Street Journal* article about their experience trying to make the transition described their search for investment backing. At first, they seemed to be flying high. "Before they even had a business plan, a firm called Snyder Communications offered them $1.5 million in services to get their company started, in return for a 10% equity stake," the article reported. They declined the deal because they were afraid of losing control to Snyder, and presumably because they figured that other better deals lay ahead.

In the summer of 2000, "After completing a rigorous application process, they were thrilled to be accepted in Springboard 2000,…a forum for women-owned companies to pitch to venture capitalists. No money came of it."

Finally, after several more false starts on the financing path, the two women "faced reality. They decided to return to what they do best: consulting."

The article concluded that the two women "got caught up in the mania that produced such advice as: Ignore your past business background when pitching to investors; it's irrelevant." One of the women observed: "We just got seduced big time."

Karma is also reflected in how you think and talk and write about the business. Here are some exercises to try to assess your own karma:

—Pretend your business has become extremely successful and you have been asked to give a speech about how you succeeded. Write a 5-10 minute speech that explains how you came to start the business, and what factors you think were most important in your past to explain your success.

—Pretend you are being interviewed by a psychologist who wants to know what personality traits it takes to successfully start your own business. Explain how your personality is appropriate.

—Spend several days doing some "journaling." Let your writing wander as you try to articulate the emotions and passion that are driving you to start this business.

When you're all done with these exercises, you'll likely know, if not specifically, then instinctively, if this business is truly right for you, and whether you can communicate the fit to the outside world. ■

Chapter 5

The Presentation:
Giving Form to Your Ideas

CHAPTER SUMMARY

Even before writing a plan, you'll want to have a presentation at the ready. Develop your presentation by putting yourself into the shoes of potential investors. Here are twelve questions that every presentation should address, along with tips on making effective presentations.

"If you can't articulate in one or two minutes of speech why you offer a compelling solution, then I question whether you in fact have a compelling solution."

—*Venture capitalist participant in survey for this book*

A t this point, you're probably wondering, when do we actually write stuff down? We've had it so well drummed into us that we've got to get a written plan together that we get itchy about writing.

One of the many problems with what we've been taught is that the preparation of the presentation comes after the writing of the business plan. This may seem logical in the context of how we think about the order of the investment process—i.e. write a plan, submit it to investors, meet to do a presentation, begin discussions, negotiate, etc.

But as I've pointed out, in the ready-fire-aim approach increasingly necessary in the investment process, writing a business plan isn't necessarily the first stage of the process. Increasingly, entrepreneurs are making presentations to investors who may or may not care whether they've seen a business plan. In my survey of venture capitalists, there was nearly unanimous agreement with this statement: "I can become intrigued by a company that I am referred to by reliable sources, even if it doesn't yet have a complete written business plan"; all except one of the 42 respondents answered affirmatively to the statement. Given their skepticism about business plans, many investors aren't necessarily upset about skipping the business plan and going right to a presentation.

So, when it comes to putting pen to paper, or mouse to computer, a formal slide presentation should be your first order of business. Aside from what's appropriate in the order of things, the presentation actually serves a number of important purposes:

- *It focuses your thinking.* It is thereby important both strategically and psychologically. You don't want to spend many hours early on writing a business plan, but you want to have a clear sense of what your business is all about. Preparing a presentation is a way to begin planning. In addressing the key issues facing the business, you accomplish a psychological mission: preparing to start realizing a specific form of your dream.
- *It prepares you for a key milestone in the investment process.* Once you begin speaking with investors, and setting up meetings, a formal presentation will be your personal introduction, your way of not only quickly explaining what you do, but letting the investors see you perform, and thus beginning to get to know you.
- *It launches the writing process.* Developing a presentation makes the eventual preparation of a written business plan, should you decide later in the business development process to do so, much easier than it would otherwise be.

Getting Ready

I suggest a very simple approach to preparing the presentation: Go through the questions investors want answered, and jot down responses to each one. Try to include both positives and negatives. When you're done, you'll not only have a presentation that will capture investors' attention, but you'll also have the beginnings of a business plan that investors will want to read.

If you're wondering whether I've included examples of presentations, the answer is no. This presentation should be unique to you, and you alone. My reasoning is the same as with the business plan—to the extent that you try to imitate someone else's presentation, you risk diluting your own. Investors tend to see lots of slide shows these days, what with various conferences at which entrepreneurs make brief presentations. They want to see unique presentations, not more of the same.

I've developed a list of twelve key questions you need to answer. They deal with the issues that investors are most concerned about. As you go through them, beginning on the next page, here are a few technical points to keep in mind as you develop your own presentation:

- **Keep it concise.** Answer the questions with one slide each, which will make the entire presentation 12 slides. Figuring that it will take you about two minutes to explain each slide, your entire presentation will be 24 minutes.
- **Stay on point.** Answer each question with approximately three to six bullet points, or brief phrases, each. If you can't capture necessary detail in bullet points or brief phrases, save it for the oral explanation you will provide for each slide.
- **Develop supporting information.** Related to the previous point, jot down notes for each slide that will serve as the basis of your discussion points to explain the slides. You don't want your presentation to be a simple recitation of the points on each slide.

Twelve Questions

1. *What is the opportunity?* Another way of asking this
question is this: What is the problem you are fixing? Many
Internet businesses—such as online car markets or travel
agencies—have been pegged to fixing an inefficient and
cumbersome market via a more open and speedy system. But
sometimes, the "problem" turns out not to have been as
serious as projected; witness the collapse of online grocery
services like Webvan and Homeruns.com. The argument of
online grocery entrepreneurs that traditional grocery store
shopping was a problem turned out to be untrue, or at least
not as true as they expected.

And if it's a new problem or opportunity, investors will
invariably wonder: Why has no one tried to fix this problem
before? Or if they did, why didn't it work? That will
certainly be a question a few years from now, when some
entrepreneurs propose a new variation of online grocery
shopping.

But there's more to answering this question than simply
demonstrating that there's an urgent problem that needs
fixing. You also need to convince potential backers that there
are huge premiums for solving the problem. This is usually
where those Forrester marketing studies get pulled out; i.e.
this market is expected to grow 250% a year for the next ten
years, and if we can capture just 1.7% of that market, we'll
all be multibillionaires.

Resist the urge to dwell on those marketing studies—
investors have come to despise them—and instead provide
data on the size of today's market, with various estimates on
potential market growth. If the marketing data is suspect, or
incomplete, say so.

2. *What gives you special advantages in solving the
problem?*

Investors refer to the competitive advantages small
businesses bring to the marketplace. The ideal competitive
advantage from their viewpoint is something proprietary—
say, a patent on a new drug or important chemical or

manufacturing process. A patent provides a form of government protection against imitators. Other proprietary advantages can come from trademarks and copyrights, though these are less desirable because they tend to be less protective for small companies. (A young company's trademark typically isn't well known, and thus less important in the marketplace than well-established corporate trademarks.) So be careful in making a huge deal out of these in your presentation.

Another kind of special advantage may be the management team's prior experience. If the management team has previously successfully developed a similar kind of complex software as is now being proposed for a new company, the team may have a potential advantage. Say so in the presentation.

Simply having "a head start on the competition" isn't usually considered all that significant—unless you have a way of creating what are known as "barriers to entry" that make it difficult for new competitors to imitate your offering. Your vast database of important Web site content, or licensing agreements you have with corporate partners, may help you create barriers to entry, and if so are worthy of mention.

3. What makes you think that the people involved in your company are especially qualified to grow this business?

This gets at the issues posed in the previous chapter. Not only is it one of the key issues investors are concerned about, but how you deal with it is especially revealing to prospective investors.

Another way of asking this question is: Why is this a business only you can do and/or why is this business right for you? It's why venture capitalists go after MIT engineers or Cal Tech scientists—they have special knowledge in especially attractive new technologies.

If you're not an accomplished university scientist, which most of us aren't, then it's incumbent on you to provide a convincing answer to this question. The best kind of answer includes evidence from past performance—not just that you started another company, but how things worked out. Many entrepreneurs gloss over this because the outcome wasn't especially clear-cut. I believe it's important to be as forthright as possible here—explain that a previous corporate management stint was cut short because of downsizing, or that another startup a team member helped launch was sold before it achieved its full potential.

Ideally, you might say something about the lessons learned from previous ventures whose outcomes were less than clear-cut, and why you think this one will be different.

Investors are extremely skeptical about the team's ability to succeed, so it's best to anticipate their skepticism, and try to answer questions before they are asked.

4. What is the model?

This question used to be posed as, What is the strategy? The word "model" became popular with the advent of the Internet, when entrepreneurs spoke about "the advertising model" or "the membership model" or "the retail model." It is really your scheme, or approach, to conducting your business and generating recurring revenues.

It's become another area of skepticism for investors because a number of models that were popular during the dot-com craze have fallen into disfavor—particularly the advertising model. Advertising on the Internet hasn't turned out to be in the same league as advertising for television or magazines.

So be careful in identifying your model to explain it carefully, and provide your assessment as to why you expect it to succeed.

5. What makes it scalable?

This refers to your ability to ramp volume up quickly with minimal additions of new people. Scalability is another of those terms that became popular during the dot-com boom because the Internet was seen as providing huge opportunities for easy scalability. For some businesses, like online auctions and travel, the Internet has turned out to be a great mechanism for achieving scalability. For other businesses, like food and toys, the Internet didn't provide the anticipated scalability.

6.*How do you know you'll have customers?* This is the question that entrepreneurs often answer most inadequately during presentations. For whatever reasons, too many entrepreneurs try to justify business based on external market studies, and neglect all they've done to identify customers and prospects.

Here you should present information of the sort encouraged in Chapter 10, "Touch the Marketplace." Investors want to know about your surveys or test marketing initiatives. They'll be sitting on the edges of their seats awaiting your evidence, and the harder that evidence is, the better. The closer you are to achieving real sales, so you can begin to show sales trends, the better.

7.*How do you connect to customers?*

This is a followup to the previous question, and relates to your methods of selling to customers and staying in contact with them. Are you going through retail channels, direct mail, using the Web, or some combination?

If you've obtained customers, do you have methods for staying in contact with them? One of the more popular, and effective, these days is regular email communication.

More significant, what evidence do you have of repeat sales? Investors are especially turned on by evidence that customers liked your product or service enough to buy more. Repeat sales can suggest that most desirable of sales situations: the annuity sale, whereby customers buy repeatedly on a long-term basis.

This is a slide you should think long and hard about. Come up with all the evidence you can about which channels seem to work best, and what you are learning about customer behavior.

8. *What is the secret for your expected sales success?*

In other words, do you have a rainmaker on board? This question is inquiring into whether you have a super salesperson on board, or a proven sales technique that can be easily taught to others. To the extent you are able to point at one or two people as having the proven ability to generate sales, you'll provide comfort to investors. They know that selling is a very special talent, and they respect it. They also know that too many young companies, technology companies in particular, don't have that talent on board, and it makes them uncomfortable.

9. *What have you learned from the competition?*

You'll notice that I haven't asked you to describe your competition. That's because investors assume everyone has competition, so saying you don't have competition will scare them.

To answer this question, think about who your competitors are, and what they do well, and what they do not do so well. To the extent you point out things they do well, and which you would like to emulate or do better, you will impress investors. The more specific you can be, the better— i.e. "One of the things that impresses us about our ABC competitor is its rigor in following up with new customers, and inquiring into their likes and dislikes. We would like to be able to do the same kind of thing, except go it one step better by responding immediately to customer dislikes."

10. *What are the risk factors?*

Every business entails risks, and as in the previous slide, to the extent you acknowledge those, you'll impress investors. This isn't an area you need to dwell on, as you should some of the market and customer matters. But you should be matter of fact that your model hasn't been well tested in your particular industry, for example, or that there is likely to be much more competition within six months than there is now. Ideally, you will provide some sense of reassurance that you appreciate the risk factors, and are attempting to confront them.

11. How will you make money?

The key issues are dealt with more fully in Chapter 7. Here you should provide a synopsis of your financial projections. But you should summarize your expectations about revenues and profits over the next few years. A key emphasis should be on your margins—profits before administrative expenses and taxes. These should be high—hopefully over 40%—but not so high that they appear unrealistic.

You should also try to anticipate the question: So, how will your margins be impacted once the competition really heats up?

12. How will you use the funds you raise?

This questions relates to the previous one, and is also discussed in greater detail in Chapter 7. Investors are more concerned than ever that their money will be used for activities that most directly generate revenues and profits. Thus, they would rather hear you itemize how investment funds will go to hire three new sales people and develop sales support literature rather than to complete research essential for product innovation.

Presentation Tips

Making a presentation is a challenge, akin to giving a speech. We all know how intimidating public speaking can be. Here are several suggestions for making the presentation come off as smoothly as possible:

- Be prepared to do variations, such as when you are given a brief amount of time—say 10 or 15 minutes max.
- Decide in advance not only who will do the presentation, but whether more than one person will be involved. Obviously you want your strongest speaker; it's generally not advisable to have more than two people doing presentations.

- Rehearse several times beforehand. This will enable you to time yourself, and will also help relax you, which will come across when you do the real presentation.
- Project a sense of openness. The business situation shouldn't all be sweetness and light. Admit to challenges and problems.
- When you discuss problems and challenges, try to convey a sense that they are not overwhelming—that you've got things under control.

Be prepared for questions, tough questions. Don't take the tough questions as expressions of doubt, but rather natural skepticism, and another chance for investors to see how you react and think.

Recycling Opportunity

The great thing about putting together this kind of presentation is that you now have a written document. Yes, an initial plan of sorts.

You can take your answers to the questions and put them in written form and, presto, you have something akin to an executive summary (the subject of the next chapter). So when prospective investors inquire as to whether you have a business plan, you can say, "We haven't completed our full plan, but we do have a brief written summary. Would you like to see that?" Invariably they do, and if they're interested in you as an investment candidate, they won't worry until they've gotten to know you much better that you don't have a full business plan.■

Chapter 6

Compose a Synopsis

CHAPTER SUMMARY

When you're asked to send along written information about your business, you should be ready with a synopsis—a brief combination of an executive summary and a publishing query. Here are seven ways to make your synopsis succeed in capturing the attention of prospective investors.

"Start with a written summary that discusses the company's history, provides current ownership structure, provides details about the market and competitors, offers a strong section on management, and finally, defensible projections."
 —Venture capitalist participant in survey for this book

T he process of raising money is invariably a combination of networking and selling (and is covered in greater detail in the chapters of Section III). But you do need to be prepared with certain written material. The previous chapter took you through the process of preparing a presentation—largely from the perspective of helping you to succinctly describe your business in a written format, but also to give you a tool for exploiting your networking and selling efforts. This chapter's purpose is similar: to take you another step down the path of assembling useful written material and to help you sell your business idea to prospective investors.

Let's say that you are contacting prospective investor candidates and trying to sell them on investing in you. Chances are you'll receive a fair number of negative responses, but what happens if you catch someone who demonstrates interest by asking you a few questions and then says, "Sounds kind of intriguing. Send me something and I'll take a look."

What is that "something?"

That "something" used to be a business plan. You'd take the 30-to-40-page document that you had slaved over for months and months, stick it in the mail, and wait for an answer. And wait, and wait, and wait some more. After all, it takes time for someone to read and digest that kind of document. If, indeed, the investor candidates actually took the time to read and digest it, which more often than not they didn't do.

Today, some entrepreneurs are still following that approach. But increasingly, savvy entrepreneurs are trying to short-circuit the process by following up with a one-to-two page synopsis of their business, often referred to simply as "the two-pager." What exactly is a synopsis?

It's difficult to define a business synopsis exactly, because there isn't a hard-and-fast formula for what it should include and for writing one. That means a synopsis can take any number of different forms, and you should feel free to put it into a format that communicates any special ideas or nuances you want to get across. One approach put forth by Peter Schmidt, an entrepreneur who has started five businesses and successfully sought out financing for them, has the synopsis answering the following investor questions:

- ξ What are you doing?
- ξ Why should I care?
- ξ Who are you, anyway?
- ξ Show me the numbers!

Important to keep in mind is that the synopsis is a written document, which means it should follow certain principles if it is to accomplish its goal of grabbing the attention of the recipient and moving him or her to a positive action of some kind. From a writing and presentation perspective, a business synopsis is kind of a cross between an executive summary in conventional business plans and a query letter in publishing. That makes it a combination informational proposal and a selling document.

Let's go through the two items I just alluded to—an executive summary and a query letter—as a way to flush out the key components of a synopsis. Then let's consider the key attributes of these items that you should focus on in your synopsis. At the end of this chapter are two models to consider when you develop your own synopsis.

An Executive Summary

An executive summary is essentially a business plan in miniature—as in two pages or less. That means it should cover the main components of a business plan—the strategy, the management team, the market, the product or service, the sales plan, and the finances, and in the process answer the questions raised for your presentation, described in the previous chapter.

But the executive summary needs to go beyond simply addressing these issues in factual format, as if hitting items on a list. It's not an abstract or an outline. Rather, it needs to integrate these items in a cohesive and convincing way—in a way that interests and stimulates the investor candidate.

I have in my previous two books on business plans recommended trying to write the executive summary in advance of writing a full plan, and that is certainly the case if you are attempting to develop a synopsis. You want to capture the essentials of your business approach in a clear written form. But once you have something akin to an executive summary written, you still need to go further in developing a synopsis you can send out to prospective investors.

A Query Letter

This is the kind of letter freelance writers use to try to convince magazine editors to give them assignments. In contrast to an executive summary, the emphasis here is less on the particulars of the idea and more on why the idea is especially relevant to the magazine (i.e. investor). In other words, its focus is on convincing and selling the recipient.

The challenge of writing an effective query letter to a magazine is to communicate the key ideas of the coming article, without actually writing the article. Thus, you need to entice the recipient with just enough *relevant* information. I emphasize the word relevant because it is easy to include lots of irrelevant information. You want to communicate that you and your team are focused on the most important priorities associated with growing your business.

The idea is to identify the key components—capture the essence of the article (i.e. business) you plan—in terms of its relevance to and impact on readers. It's a proposal for why your article will be worth the money and space the publication will invest.

A book popular with freelance writers, *How to Write Irresistible Query Letters*, by Lisa Collier Cool, identifies three key components of an effective query letter: the lead, summary, and author's biography. The lead is the first paragraph of your synopsis and, as Cool says, it "must pack a powerful wallop, or you may lose the sales fight in the first round. The right lead will not only capture and hold a busy editor's interest, but it will vividly introduce your topic and slant." She advises that it must be packed with specifics, assembled in an interesting format.

While a business synopsis needn't show the same polish as a magazine query letter—you're selling a business concept, not your attributes as a professional writer—the point about packaging and specifics are well taken.

Bringing the Two Together

In writing your synopsis, then, you need to combine the best of an executive summary and a query letter into a written communication that will grab the prospective investor's attention and make him or her want to pick up the phone and call you to set up a meeting to learn more about possibly investing in your business. Here are a number of key requirements for a successful synopsis:

1.   ***Keep it brief.*** This means two pages or less. It's much more difficult to write concisely than in more verbose fashion. So while there might be a temptation to send a detailed four-to-five-page summary, resist that temptation.

2.   ***Stand out from the crowd.*** Remember that the investor candidates are being deluged with ideas and proposals. Much like editors who peruse query letters, investors are overwhelmed, and thus somewhat cynical. They know they will judge most of the proposals they read as worthless to them. At the same time, they know they need to be alert to that diamond in the rough, that one-in-a-hundred that will be worth their time, and money. You need to stand out as that diamond in the rough.

3.   ***Stay on point.*** Stick with the key attributes of your business that you feel will lead to marketplace success. These are many of the same points you will have highlighted in your presentation—evidence that customers will buy, of attractive profit margins, the ability to achieve scale, and the power of the management team.

4.   ***Sell without being overly promotional.*** What you really want to do is sell the prospective investor without the person realizing he or she has been sold. It's a subtle trait of effective writing—to present the facts in such a compelling way that they move the reader to take action. It's something that successful direct mail pieces do very well. It's usually accomplished by highlighting the most compelling facts about the business and its accomplishments to date.

5.   ***Make it hard hitting.*** You want to show confidence that you can accomplish what you are setting out to accomplish. That requires that you show off your accomplishments to date—with a pat on the back to you and your team by briefly noting the difficulty of any of your accomplishments. (i.e. In a down market for telecommunications equipment, ABC Telecom has already shown a 50% sales increase this year over last year.) In

looking toward the future, state to this effect: Here's what we *will* do, not what we *hope* to do. In other words, your synopsis must exude confidence.

6. ***Think in terms of themes.*** In a one-to-two-page document in which you are trying to communicate a great deal of information, you want to avoid the danger of including too much data. One way to do that is to ask yourself this question: What are the two or three most important things we want the investor prospect to get out of this letter? Once you do that, you will likely find yourself eliminating extraneous information.

7. ***Capture your thought process.*** This is perhaps the most difficult thing to accomplish. But it relates to the points I made in Chapter 5, about your karma. The synopsis should capture not only the key business facts around your venture, but its "personality" and the intangibles that you and other members of your team bring to the table that will make it successful long term. For example, if you have determined that a key to your venture's long-term success is selling directly to end users in an industry that is dominated by middlemen, you might explain that you have decided that, despite the difficulties, you want to be closer to the ultimate customer than your competitors are able to get. Perhaps there are ongoing communication channels you will be able to exploit, that will serve you more effectively in the long run. Allude to these, and provide any specifics you can of how you've already begun enhancing the communication process.

An Example

I've included here an example of an effective synopsis on page 77. While I have shied away from using illustrations of key planning items because of my feeling that they should be unique to each business, I know that the synopsis is particularly mysterious to many entrepreneurs. This one is a letter by a Massachusetts entrepreneur I know, Steve Snyder who used his as the launching pad for his company, Centerstone Software of Westwood, MA, to raise

$4 million of investment funds in 2001—one of the most difficult years for raising investment funds in the last 40 years.

While the first paragraph of Centerstone's synopsis appears to me to have some weaknesses—most notably too much jargon (i.e. "core platform of solutions")—it fulfills the key requirement of including the most compelling information. It provides a big-picture view of the product's functions and market—that the company's software helps companies maximize the effectiveness of space allocation, building operations, maintenance, and other such functions. The letter might have made some allusion to the savings that such maximization makes possible, but chances are most venture investors know that expenses associated with corporate facilities can be substantial, and that controlling them is a slice right out of so-called "G&A," or general-and-administrative expenses that adversely affect profit margins. It also notes a very important advantage that the company possesses: a Term Sheet, or commitment for part of the sought-after investment from a venture capital firm.

The next four paragraphs hit on three key points for Centerstone, and represent an excellent example of identifying a few key themes and sticking to them. First, that it is "vendor neutral," which means that Centerstone isn't limited only to software it develops. Second, a sense of the enormity of the market opportunity. And third, and perhaps most significant, that Centerstone has customers—and a significant pipeline of new prospects.

Your Synopsis

You want this both to sing, and to sing in your voice. The key to achieving that is to rewrite, rewrite, and rewrite some more. Put a draft down on paper and let it sit a day or two. Then go back to it with a fresh eye. After you've revised several times, pass a draft around to your partner(s) and/or management team. Try it out on members of your board of directors, or advisory board, or any other "friends" of your company. Once you have something you feel good about, begin sending it out to prospective investors. Take note of the reactions and questions you get back. Feel free to adjust and revise some more. After all, your synopsis is, and always will be, a work in progress. ■

Synopsis Example

Fred,

Centerstone is an Internet ASP delivering **e-Center One**[(tm)], a core platform of solutions that enable Corporate-wide management and their outsourced service vendors to efficiently use all Workplace resources, including Real Estate, Building Operation, Space Planning, Leasing, Work Order and Maintenance, and others. Blue Chip Venture has given us a Term Sheet and we are presently looking for additional investment of $2-3 million in order to complete the round.

The most important element of our e-Center One architecture is our "core value": The Data and Mapping Engine. Centerstone enables the INTEGRATION of multiple applications onto the e-Center One PLATFORM for the **Workplace Management community**. This vendor-neutral platform model is the key to Centerstone's valuation potential. Centerstone will provide a platform that enables convergence of data, applications and service resources for managing Corporate Workplace infrastructure over the Internet on a continual-use basis. Centerstone just happened to originate out of the one-application facilities management market, but that narrow focus is not where we have directed the Company and as a platform we have already graduated beyond those old limitations using e-Center One. We will offer other best of breed applications (asset management, lease management, preventive maintenance and work order, hazardous waste recording and reporting) to the Workplace Management community from our platform.

The market opportunity is enormous. Our target is the $157B in annual office operating costs that are excess costs or waste, incurred by U.S. companies that have revenues of $50M or more. This group of companies, which is greater than 20,000 in number, spends $505B annually on Office Operational Costs. It is important to note that these amounts EXCLUDE the purchase of any product (Furniture, Fixtures or Equipment), any additional costs related to outsourcing any of the measured functions or activities, or any costs of design, engineering or construction.

We now have 14 new e-Center One customers: **Northpoint Communications, Manugistics, Pearson Education** (they own Simon & Schuster and Prentice Hall), **Silverstream, Tufts Health Plan, Raychem, Digitas, Aspen Technology** and the **Mass Medical Society,** and **PeopleSoft, Commerce One** and **Remedy Corporation** (through Relocation Connections, one of our West Coast partners), **Wheelhouse** (through Cresa Partners, one of our East Coast partners) and **Sovereign Bank** (through Fox Relocation, another of our East Coast partners). And we fully expect several others to close shortly.

As a result of this activity and the development of a sales pipeline for e-Center One subscriptions (we have more than 70 sales prospects in the e-Center One pipeline -- all without spending any marketing dollars and without a sales force), we are closing e-Center One business a full business quarter ahead of our original schedule.

Hopefully this has given you a good idea for our excitement. We would very much like to meet in person and give you a product demo.

I look forward to hearing from you.

Steve Snyder

Chapter 7

Develop Meaningful and Hard-Hitting Financials

CHAPTER SUMMARY
The bad news: investors still require financial projections. The good news: today's financial projections are less onerous, and more big-picture in orientation. Here is guidance on how to make your financial projections conventional, brief, financially informed and up to date. Be prepared to provide your rationale for past, current and future expenditures and financial requirements. Sample statements are provided.

"Start with the financial projections, then back into the business plan."
—Venture capitalist participant in survey for this book

There is one remnant of the traditional business plan that hasn't gone away in the protocol for obtaining financing—financial projections. Unfortunately, this is the aspect of business planning that many entrepreneurs find most difficult and tedious.

The good news is that in today's climate of high anxiety and investors' focus on getting to the key essentials as quickly as possible, the financials you need to develop are a streamlined version of what used to be required.

In the bad old days of business planning, the emphasis was on completeness and thoroughness. Thus, you were encouraged to provide detailed financial projections looking ahead at least three years, and preferably five years. This meant trying to project all your expenses like office rent and travel expenses and marketing brochures, along with revenue sources.

The main problem with such requirements was that they were unrealistic, and became increasingly unrealistic as the business climate became less predictable, and faster moving. There are few entrepreneurs whose detailed financial projections three, four, or five years into the future could be considered to be meaningful.

Some investors continue to request such completeness, under the theory that it's not the financial projections themselves that are important, but the exercise of making forecasts that entrepreneurs are forced to go through. Increasingly, though, investors pay little heed to long-range financial forecasts, and may even regard them with some disdain. They view these spreadsheets through the same lens through which they view the upbeat expectations detailed in many written business plans—as exercises in fantasy.

This process isn't a matter of intellectual debate, though. The financial projections are central to determining a company's current and future value, and thus how much a company a particular investment buys. Thus, financial projections tend to be discounted heavily by investor's intent on driving down the price they pay for a company's stock.

What counters these investor efforts more effectively than the formalistic three-to-five-year forecasts is a focused—and reality-based—effort to project a company's financial status, no matter how far into the future you are projecting. The real goal here is to demonstrate to investors that you have command of your venture's finances, and that you will maximize the usefulness of the cash they put in. Sometimes less is more. Remember, investors are anxious. They want you to provide them with concreteness and certainty in a totally uncertain world. Your challenge is to reassure them, and one of the best ways to do that is with convincing numbers.

The Financial Package

There are three main components to an effective summary of your company's financial expectations. What's important to keep in mind here is that they shouldn't be treated as entirely separate components. Rather, they should build one off the other and be integrated. This chapter explains each component, and how each leads one into the other. It then provides examples of the third component, which illustrates integration of the first two, courtesy of a nationally known financial consultant to growing companies.

1. Establish Milestones

Most of us are procrastinators. Give us the chance, and we'll delay our various obligations, at work and at home. That's the investor rationale for wanting to see a list of key milestones—to force you into not only establishing tangible goals, but setting dates for completing the goals.

What kind of milestones am I talking about? Generally speaking, these are milestones that cost you something to accomplish, or bring in sales or other revenue, which explains why this advice is grouped in the financial area. For example, various milestones might be attached to development of your company's first product. These might include:

ξ Finalize design
ξ Complete a beta version
ξ Test the performance of the beta version
ξ Make product adjustments based on the tests
ξ Write documentation
ξ Begin production of complete product

As a follow on, various milestones might then be attached to marketing the product, including installation at three test sites (prospective customers), hiring and training sales people, developing marketing literature, building a Web site, and so forth. For the record, you would want to assign a date to each task—ideally a date that you feel is very doable.

Treat your milestone list almost as you would a written contract with an important customer or partner. You should expect that you will be held accountable to your milestones. Once you show your list of milestones to

81

prospective investors, they will want to know where you are in the process of completing each of them. If any of the milestone dates have passed between the time you contacted the investors and actually met with them, they will almost certainly want to know whether you achieved the milestones, and when. Answers like, "We're real close to meeting that one," or "Oh, we're adjusting that one because of some supplier issues" won't help your case. Investors will think to themselves: If these people can't meet their goals while they are trying to impress us to get money, how well will they do once they have our money safely deposited in their bank accounts?

For your own internal financial planning purposes, you will want to assign costs to accomplishing each milestone. That will help you in the next two stages.

2. Identify Sources and Uses of Funds

Prospective investors will almost always ask you these two questions:

--How much money are you looking for?

--What are you going to do with the money?

While investors have asked these two questions since the beginning of time, it seems, it is in our current age of high anxiety that they appear to have become nearly obsessively concerned about how you answer these questions. There are wrong answers and right answers to these questions.

Your answer to the first question tells them if you are thinking about the growth challenge realistically enough. If you are seeking what they feel to be "too little" money to achieve your milestones, they will question your overall savviness. Your protestations that you are trying to "be conservative" won't count for much. Professional investors who have had experience in a particular industry have a good idea of the financial requirements necessary to grow a company in that industry from one stage to another. If you are seeking too little money, in their estimation, then you will have created "macro" doubts—concerns about your understanding of the big picture.

One other thing that investors want to know in your answer to this first question is that you have considered other sources of money than the investors themselves. It always helps your case if you have other investors potentially committed to provide some of the targeted funds. Thus, if you need $3 million of investment funds over the next two years, it could be that you have a commitment of $500,000 from the angel investors who gave you startup funds a year back, and you're seeking another $2.5 million from venture capitalists.

If you pass the test regarding the first question, then you move on to the even tougher second question. Here, investors don't really want to hear that you are going to spend the money on growing the company. Rather, they want to learn specifically how the money they provide will be used to create revenues, expand market share, and rapidly increase shareholder value.

Thus, the following answer won't carry you very far: "We need $1 million of investment funds this year and $2 million next year, and we will be using the money to complete our product development to get into the marketplace, and for general and administrative expenses."

No, investors today want specifics, lots of specifics.

Which of the items on your Milestones list will you be spending investment money to achieve, and how much? To the extent you can show revenues, you do yourself a favor, since investors increasingly want evidence that you have a real business, not just a total startup.

Thus, it may be that you still have some funds left over from initial angel financing based on better-than-expected sales of a product or service, or you've generated some consulting revenues related to your main product or service. The best scenario is to show actual customer revenues related to the core business for which you are seeking new investor funds—for example, revenues from advance orders on a product or service. As I've noted previously, investors are looking for evidence of customer interest, and obviously the best expression of customer interest is hard cash.

The idea in your list of uses for the funds is to be able to show investor money being targeted at key revenue-producing milestones. For example, it's preferable to show investment funds being used to hire a sales management pro and the first few members of the sales team, rather than hiring an office manager and completing product documentation.

To the extent that you can quantify how much of the investment funds will go to specific milestones, you will enhance your cause. Everyone knows that money you receive from customers will be mingled with investment funds. The idea here is to demonstrate that there are significant revenue-producing milestones that won't be completed as scheduled without the designated investment funds.

3. Provide Key Financial Projections

This is where you pull together the numbers to support three questions that press most heavily on the minds of investors:

ξ   How much financing will you really need?
ξ   What can your revenues, and compound annual growth rate (CAGR), be over the next several years?
ξ   When will you break even?

To answer these questions, you will need a set of integrated financial forecasts that look ahead at least three years; these forecasts include an income statement, cash flow statement, and balance sheet. In contrast to the traditional approach, such forecasts aren't detailed monthly or quarterly numbers, but rather annual revenue and expense numbers that provide a sense of your company's expected size and growth rate. You should do the first-year's numbers on a monthly basis, though you need not include this information in the materials you initially make available to prospective investors; the idea here is to think through what you will spend to meet each of your milestones.

These numbers need to be backed up with an explanation of the major assumptions you applied in arriving at the numbers. The revenue growth in years one to three should be explainable by two factors:

ξ   Your capturing a meaningful share of the market early in the market's life cycle.

ξ   A comparison to what other early-stage companies have accomplished in the revenue arena.

Your anticipated expenses (sales and marketing, research and development, general and administrative, cost of goods, etc.) should be comparable to what other companies have spent. (You can typically determine what other companies spent by searching out Securities and Exchange Commission Form S-1's, which are filed by companies when they go public.)

Samples of the annual financial projections, key associated measurements (staffing, revenue analysis, etc.), and of the assumptions underlying the numbers are provided at the end of this chapter, courtesy of Michael Gonnerman, a professional financial adviser to many smaller growing companies. His financial templates and statements can be downloaded at www.gonnerman.com. For further direction on the specifics of preparing detailed financial statement, see my previous book on business plans, *How to* Really *Create a Successful Business Plan* (Inc. Publishing.

Putting It Together

The goal for your financials is to provide prospective investors with quick insights into both your company's financial health and your financial thinking. Successfully accomplishing these goals requires that you tend to the technical requirements described previously, as well as effectively packaging your information. Here are some guidelines for effectively packaging your financials

ξ   ***Keep them conventional.*** This means using commonly understood accounting language to identify items, and arranging them in the accepted order. Put all the dollar numbers in millions, and don't attempt to show the numbers out to an exact dollar amount, since this implies you can forecast that well months and years into the future. You'll see the right way for setting up your tables in the examples at the end of this chapter.

ξ   ***Keep them brief.*** Remember, the idea here isn't to create a business plan, it is to enable prospective investors to quickly understand the company's key financial issues and outlook. So confine your milestones and sources/uses of funds to one page each. Allow two to four pages for income and cash flow statements, and at least that much for an explanation of your underlying assumptions. Your projections should look ahead at least three (and up to five) years on an annual basis. If the company has had ongoing operations, then you might go back one year with a detailed statement, and include brief summaries of prior years—possibly even limiting them to a graphical format, to show the overall trends of revenues and profits/losses.

ξ   ***Involve a financial expert.*** As I indicated at the start of this chapter, putting together financial reports isn't fun for most entrepreneurs. That is why I strongly recommend you involve a financial expert to help put the report together or, at the least, review what you've done yourself. It is easy to make errors in terminology and organization of your financials, and a financial expert can help you spot problems. The last thing you want is for prospective investors to be pointing out problems.

ξ   ***Keep the information up-to-date.*** At all costs, don't send out projections that include three or four months that have already passed. Then prospective investors will rightfully wonder: How did your actual results come out? If they didn't meet the projections, you've sown the seeds of doubt in two ways: First, you weren't on top of things enough and, second, you didn't do what you said you would do.

ξ   ***Be prepared to explain the rationale behind your expenditures.*** Investors want to be sure that a company's leaders were engaged in the preparation of financials. Thus, you should be prepared for questions about particular items in the financial projections. Why, for example, are you allocating such a large amount for sales training? You want to be able to offer more than the general answer: "We want our sales force to be the best trained around." You want to also be able to point to specifics, such as the importance in your particular industry of having highly professional sales training literature. Or the question could come up on the other side as well; for example, why do your administrative expenses seem so low? You might then want to answer that you have decided to hire only a part-time office administrator, in the interests of being able to apportion more funds to sales training.

ξ   ***Reveal your financials to prospective investors as appropriate.*** You are under no obligation when you speak with a prospective investor who requests that

87

you send written material along to include your financial projections with your synopsis. As I discuss elsewhere, I prefer to dole out company information in small pieces. If the prospective investor's curiosity is piqued by your synopsis, he or she will likely request some financial information. At this point, you can explain that you have a list of milestones, source/uses of funds, and financial projections.

In sum, then, the idea behind your financials isn't to overwhelm prospective investors, but rather to communicate the financial essentials about your business in the most concise and easy-to-understand ways possible. ④

SOFTWARE, INC.
INCOME STATEMENT
for years ending Dec. 31 (000 omitted)

Revenues	2003	2004	2005	2006	2007
Product	4,400	7,000	10,400	16,200	25,000
Services	1,100	2,145	3,600	8,800	15,000
	5,500	9,145	14,000	25,000	40,000
Cost of revenues	1,200	1,634	2,240	3,500	4,800
Gross margin	4,300	7,511	11,760	21,500	35,200
Operating expenses					
Sales & Marketing	2,340	4,476	6,720	11,750	18,400
Research & Development	1,081	1,742	2,520	4,250	6,40
Finance & Administration	639	1,004	1,540	2,500	3,200
	4,060	7,222	10,780	18,500	28,000
Operating income (loss)	240	289	980	3,000	7,200
Non-operating income					
(expense)	-26	11	74	90	135
Income (loss) before taxes	214	300	1,054	3,090	7,335
Income tax expense	-1	-1	-1	-1,250	-2,934
Net income	213	299	1,053	1,840	4,401

CASH FLOW STATEMENTS
for years ending Dec. 31

	2003	2004	2005	2006	2007
Cash provided by (used in) operating activities					
Collections from customers	4,921	9,015	13,460	23,776	38,330
Payments	-5,036	-8,693	12,462	22,109	34,233
	-115	322	997	1,667	4,097
Cash used in investing activities	-145	-265	-465	-665	-865
Cash provided by (used in) financing activities					
Bank	0	0	0	0	0
Capital lease proceeds	107	135	100	200	240
Capital lease payments	-53	-82	-117	-75	-116
Investors	0	2,050	0	0	0
	54	3,003	-17	125	124
Total cash flow	-206	3,060	515	1,127	3,356
Ending cash balance	384	3,444	3959	5,086	8,443

Michael Gonnerman, www.gonnerman.com

89

SOFTWARE, INC.
BALANCE SHEETS
as of Dec. 31 (000 omitted)

Current assets	2002	2003	2004	2005	2006	2007
Cash	590	384	3,444	3,959	5,086	8,443
Accounts receivable	302	1,440	2,308	3,533	6,309	10,095
	892	1,824	5,752	7,493	11,396	18,538
Fixed assets	116	197	302	666	1,109	1,604
Other assets	67	109	129	129	129	129
	1,075	2,130	6,183	8,288	12,624	20,271
Capital leases— current portion	33	66	117	75	116	157
Account payable and accrued expenses	165	515	817	1,201	2,030	3,026
Deferred revenues	404	840	1,290	1,975	3,527	5,642
	602	1,421	2,224	3,251	5,672	8,826
Long term debt— capital leases	101	124	125	150	234	317
	703	1,545	2,349	3,401	5,906	9,143
Equity (Deficit)						
Common stock and paid in surplus	2,147	2,147	5,097	5,097	5,097	5,097
Accumulated losses	-1,775	-1,562	-1,263	-210	1,630	6,032
	372	585	3,834	4,887	6,727	11,129
	1,075	2,130	6,183	8,288	12,634	20,271

Michael Gonnerman, www.gonnerman.com

SOFTWARE, INC.
STAFFING
as of Dec. 31

	2002	2003	2004	2005	2006	2007
Sales & Marketing	9	15	26	36	58	75
Customer services	7	15	18	27	40	65
Research & Dev.	8	12	17	22	32	50
General & Admin.	4	6	9	15	20	30
	28	48	70	100	150	220

STATISTICS

	2003	2004	2005	2006	2007
Operations					
Revenues per employee ($000)	115	131	140	167	182
Expenses per employee ($000)	110	127	130	147	149
Cost of revenues as a % of revenues	22%	18%	16%	14%	12%
Financing					
Financing from new investors (net) ($000)	0	2,950	0	0	0
Balance sheet DSO	50	60	60	60	60
Working capital ($000)	403	3,528	4,242	5,723	9,712

% of REVENUE ANALYSIS
for the years ending Dec. 31

Revenues	2003	2004	2005	2006	2007
Product	80%	77%	74%	65%	63%
Services	20%	23%	26%	35%	38%
	100%	100%	100%	100%	100%
Cost of revenues	22%	18%	16%	14%	12%
Gross margin	78%	82%	84%	86%	88%
Operating expenses					
Sales & Marketing	43%	49%	48%	47%	46%
Research & Dev.	20%	19%	18%	17%	16%
Finance & Admin.	12%	11%	11%	10%	8%
	74%	79%	77%	74%	70%
Operating income (loss)	4%	3%	7%	12%	18%

Michael Gonnerman, www.gonnerman.com

SOFTWARE, INC.
ASSUMPTIONS UNDERLYING
FINANCIAL PROJECTIONS 2002 -- 2007

BASIS OF PRESENTATION

The Company's principal operating objective is to dominate the object oriented programming market. Revenues are projected to increase at a 64% rate annually, to $40 million in 2007, with earnings at 11%:

	2003	2004	2005	2006	2007
Revenues	5	9	14	25	40
Net Income (loss)	.2	.3	1.1	1.9	4.4

To finance this growth the Company requires a $3 million financing in Q1 2003. This financing would enable the Company to develop a world-class Board of Directors, to strengthen the management team and to provide for:

ξ increases in sales staffing in North America;
ξ an expansion of the international distributor program;
ξ a strategic partner development program;
ξ increases in spending on marketing programs; and,
ξ the development staffing necessary to rewrite the product in C++ and to accelerate the introduction of additional product features.

After this financing the Company's cash balances in 2004 and 2005 will range between $3.4 and $4.0 million, which provides operating cushion. In addition, it may enable management to grow the business by acquiring companies with related technologies.

SUMMARY OF ASSUMPTIONS

The accompanying financial projections are based on a number of assumptions made by the management concerning future events and circumstances. The assumptions disclosed below are those which management considers to be significant to the preparation of its financial projections. Some assumptions, regardless of the amount of study or analysis, will not materialize, and unexpected events and circumstances may occur after the date of the financial projections. Thus, it should be expected that actual results will vary, to some degree, from the projected results and the variations could be material.

Operations: 2002 -- 2007

1. The projections include actual results through July 2002, and are supported by monthly projections for the remainder of 2002, quarterly projections for 2003 and annual projections for 2004 - 2007.
2. Revenues will increase from $5.5 million in 2003 to $40 million in 2007, which represents a 64% annual growth rate.
3. The focus on service revenues (training, maintenance and consulting) will increase service revenues from 20% of total revenues in 2003 to 38% in 2007.
4. During the same period, spending on R&D will decrease from 20% of revenues to 16%, sales and marketing will

remain at approximately 43%-49%, and G&A will reduce from 12% to 8%.

Operations: 2003 Details

1. Sales rep productivity for 2003 is projected at 80% of quota ($1,000,000 of billings per rep per year), which compares to 85% for 2002.
2. Spending on controllable marketing programs increases from $.4 million in 2002 to $1.1 million in 2003.
3. The client services staff generates training and consulting revenues (at $1,000 per day) at 43% of available capacity.
4. The Company continues to charge maintenance at 15% of license fees.
5. Staffing increases from 48 in 2003 to 70 in 2004.
6. New hires are added at 6/quarter, with recruiting fees averaging $9,000 - $10,000 per new hire. Significant hires include: in Q1 2003 the business development manager; in Q2, a CFO; and, in Q4 the managing director for Pacific Rim sales. New hires are assumed to begin the first day of the quarter (overstates salary expense -- this provide for the cost of attrition, which is not accounted for separately).
7. Annual salaries (except sales staff) increase 4% in April 2003.
8. DSO increases to 50 days at December 2003. Management expects DSO to increase as international and service billings increase, and have increased DSO to 60 days in 2004.
9. Accounts payable are paid in 30 days, commissions in 60 days and profit sharing in the first month of the following quarter.

10. Interest expense for capital leases is provided at 20%, and interest income on deposits is earned at 2%.
11. Depreciation is calculated using the straight-line method over 3 years.
12. Federal income taxes are provided at 34% and state income taxes are provided at 9.5%. Management anticipates the $1.8 million of net operating loss carry-forwards at 2002 will be available to offset the Federal and state income tax provisions, and is reviewing this with its tax accountants. A change in ownership may limit the amount available for any year.
13. The Company is currently leasing 12,900 sq. ft. at $20/foot (gross), and expects to move in Q3 2003 to new offices (20,000 sq. ft. at $24/foot).

Investing 2003 -- 2007

1. Equipment purchases are projected at $.1 million in 2003, $.3 million in 2004, $.5 million in 2005, $.7 million in 2006 and $.9 million in 2007.

Financing 2003 -- 2007

1. In Q1 2003 the Company raises $3 million of equity financing; after $50,000 of legal expenses, $2.95 million is available to fund operating and financing cash flow requirements.
2. The Company anticipates financing approximately 30% of its equipment purchases with capital equipment lease financing in 2003 - 2007.

3. There are no provisions for bank loans, accounts receivable financing or additional loans from stockholders.

SIGNIFICANT RESULTS

Income Statement

1. Revenues increase from $5.5 million in 2003 to $40 million in 2007.
2. The Company is profitable every year.
3. The Company earns 18% pre tax in 2007 ($7.2 million on revenues of $40 million).

Cash Flow

1. Cash flows from operations are $(.1) million negative in 2003, $.3 million in 2004, and approximately $1 million, $1.7 million and $4 million in 2005, 2006 and 2007.
2. Equipment purchases total $.1 million in 2002, and increase $.2 million annually thereafter, to $.9 million in 2007.
3. During 2003 the Company's cash balances at the end of each quarter will average $3.3 million. This approximates 6 months of expenses in Q1 and 5 months of expenses in Q4.

Balance Sheet

1. At December 31, 2003,
    - ξ accounts receivable, $1.4 million, represent 50 days billings;
    - ξ working capital is $.4 million;
    - ξ long term debt totals $.1 million; and,

ξ   equity totals $.6 million.
2. At December 31, 2004:
    ξ   accounts receivable, $2.3 million, represent 60 days billings;
    ξ   working capital is $3.6 million; and,
    ξ   during 2004 equity has increased $3.2 million, to $3.8 million, reflecting the 2004 equity investment ($2.9, after legal costs) and profits of $.3 million.

SENSITIVITY

The projected December 31, 2003, cash balance of $.4 million is sensitive to a number of assumptions, such as the following:

1. a $.5 million shortfall in Q4 2003 revenues would reduce cash at December 31, 2003, $.2 million;
2. an increase in days sales outstanding from 50 days to 60 days would reduce cash $.3 million;
3. paying the profit sharing in December, rather than January, would further reduce cash $.1 million.

Under this set of assumptions cash at December 31, 2003, would be reduced $.6 million, and the Company would need additional equity or borrowings in order to have a positive cash balance.

Chapter 8

Build a Web Site That Demonstrates Your Business Model

CHAPTER SUMMARY
Building an effective Web site can wow potential investors as no business plan can, since it is the first thing most prospective investors examine when they learn about a new business. Here are three possible Web design scenarios, depending on the type of business you are starting. Treat investor visitors to your site as you would customers, to communicate your business model and sales approach.

"Demonstrate for me the adaptability of your business model."
—Venture capitalist participant in survey for this book

N ot long ago, a group of entrepreneurs seeking investment funds asked me for help in revising their business plan and putting together a presentation for investors. The business they were proposing to launch was potentially quite significant: an online system for enabling insurance companies to carry out the tedious process of claim adjustments. While other areas of the insurance process had been modernized over the years, this one had remained mired in paper-based systems involving small localized claims adjustors.

The first thing I did was the first thing any prospective investor would likely do: I went to look at this startup company's Web site. After all, if the entrepreneurs were starting an online business, I wanted to see how they presented themselves online.

What I discovered was essentially a "placeholder"—a one-page Web site with the name and address of the company and some marketing lingo. When I asked one of the founders why the Web site wasn't developed, he demurred. "We wanted to get our business plan in tip-top shape. We'll be getting to the Web site after that."

I had to break the bad news to him that he was unlikely to get very far on the investment front, no matter how well done the business plan might be, until he had something much more substantive on the Web site. Ideally, visitors to the site should be able to experience the process, even if only in demonstration form.

In this day and age, the first thing business people do when they hear about an interesting new supplier or customer is that they search out the company's Web site. Investors are no different. And if a prospective company is basing its proposed business on the Web, and doesn't have a presentable Web site, it is really shooting itself in the foot.

In other words, an effective Web site may be much more important than a business plan. An effective Web site can wow investors to the point that they'll accept a delay in completing a business plan. But if your business has a heavy Web component, a well-done business plan can't compensate for the absence of a Web site.

There are reams of advice about how to develop an effective small-business Web site—via online articles and books—and I don't want to repeat that information here. My goal is to provide guidance for developing a site that will help you advance your chances with prospective investors.

Remember, the goal here is communication. And the Internet is a wonderful tool for communicating all kinds of wonderful things. A *New Yorker* cartoon a few years back captured this idea perfectly: It showed a dog typing at a computer keyboard, saying to another dog, "On the Internet, no one knows you're a dog." So it can be for you. On the Internet, no one knows you're a startup or early-stage business.

Typical Scenarios

When it comes to developing a Web site that will impress investors, one size doesn't fit all. You need a Web site that serves your company's particular needs for showcasing its expertise. Nor is the urgency for a Web site equally acute. A business that expects to sell primarily on the Internet needs a Web site more urgently than one that will be selling mostly via non-electronic outlets. Here are three types of business situations, and approaches for developing an Internet strategy for each:

1. It's an Internet-based business.

That was the situation for this chapter's opening example. The company's business model was not only a potentially innovative approach to dealing with an area of insurance, it was based entirely on the Internet.

This turns out to be kind of a double whammy. The insurance industry isn't known as one that latches easily onto innovation, so the entreprencurs needed to convince investors that the industry would indeed welcome this particular innovation. In addition, they needed to demonstrate that the whole thing would work on the Internet.

That's why these entrepreneurs needed something pretty impressive to show on the Internet. What you don't want to do is what most of the companies whose business plans were quoted in Chapter 1 did—describe a new marketing approach or a complex production model—and then have nothing for investors to review online. To say you'll construct the Web site after you get investment funds isn't the right answer.

It could be you'll complete construction of the Web site after you raise money. Possibly the idea is so compelling you can get money in advance of putting something online. To the extent that you can show investors how it will work online, you'll help yourself.

But it's expensive, you say. Perhaps the site is dependent on complex databases or massive amounts of difficult-to-obtain content. To the extent you can put *something* together, you show ingenuity and an ability to get things done.

That something may be a demonstration or a partial iteration of what you envision. Investors are forgiving if you don't necessarily have all the bells-and-whistles you have in mind, so long as they can begin to see the site taking shape via a prototype.

One early-stage company involved in using the Internet to distribute discount coupons online on behalf of retailer client subscribers constructed a site with just three client subscribers. So pretty much whatever zip code or category a visitor chose (travel, food, clothing, etc.), one or another of the three subscribers came up. But the important thing was that investors could see the concept taking shape in a very tangible way.

2. The Internet is one of several marketing or sales channels.

For many businesses, the Internet is one of several outlets. For software, clothing, food, and other such products sold also via brick-and-mortar outlets or printed catalogues, the Internet may not be central to the company's overall success.

Still and all, the company should plan for a Web site fairly early in its development process—the importance of the Internet as a channel should affect the exact timing. Among the issues that need to be addressed in showing how the Internet works are the following:

How this channel works. Just as in the case of a company entirely dependent on the Web, the business model needs to be clear. How are orders placed? When are they delivered? What are the prices?

How this channel compares to the company's other channels. In clear language, the site should explain to users its benefits in price, convenience, customer service, etc.

What the other channels are. Where else is the product sold? You may want to include other retail locations. Is it possible to order online and pick up or return the product via one of these other channels? This is a particularly important issue for products sold via retail.

3. The Internet is a promotional vehicle.

For many businesses, professional service businesses in particular, the Internet isn't an actual sales channel. In such situations, the Internet presence may be able to wait until the business is well established, though its importance as a promotional vehicle is often more significant than entrepreneurs realize.

I was heavily involved in two professional service businesses—an Internet direct marketing agency and a full-service Internet marketing agency—that required investor support, and my partners and I agonized a great deal about our Web site. In certain respects, it's more difficult to put up a promotional Web site than one that actually allows customers to buy.

Among the questions we had to deal with: What should be the tone of seriousness? What should be the mood we communicate via our design? How much razzle-dazzle design do we try to show off? How much information do we provide about our methodology? We wanted to communicate what we did, but we didn't want to communicate proprietary information that competitors might expropriate. How do we communicate our expertise? How many of our people's biographies do we provide on the site?

These and other questions were mostly matters of judgment. As a first step in making sound judgments, we visited the Web sites of our chief competitors. This provided us with some ideas; for example, a couple of them did an excellent job of linking to every single article on the Web that mentioned their company. So we decided to make that an important feature of our site, since in the professional service business, media articles mentioning your company provide significant credibility.

On the other hand, we wanted to be careful and not adopt too much of a "me, too" approach. We wanted to be sure to communicate our distinctiveness. One way we came up with to do that was to provide detailed case histories of our client engagements—with an emphasis on accomplishments. How had clients increased their own sales, or attracted more prospects?

We also wanted to find ways to encourage visitors to return to our site and keep up with our expanding expertise and accomplishments. A company that sells products and/or services right from the site has a built-in way to do that—when customers return to order again. One way we determined to do that was to launch a newsletter about trends in online Internet marketing. Our Internet site became a place where visitors could sign up for the newsletter, or actually read the contents on the site. When they received the newsletter, they would be reminded about who we were.

What Every Web Site Must *Accomplish*

No matter which of the above three categories your company is in, there are certain things that are de rigueur for a Web site in today's world—things that investors will be sensitive to, and that may turn them off if the issues aren't tended to. Here are some of those key items:

- *Develop the Web site as if you are talking directly to customers.* Yes, you want to impress investors. And it may be that you don't even have customers yet. But your Web site should talk to visitors as if they are customers— welcoming them, describing your products and/or services, and instructing them about how to purchase. This is the language investors understand best.
- *Clearly describe what the business does.* It should be immediately obvious when a visitor comes to your site what your business does. If your company specializes in corporate catering in the Cleveland metropolitan area, with an emphasis on healthful foods, then say so, via words, pictures, and customer endorsements. The worst thing you

can do is confuse visitors with vague or misleading language—especially high-sounding but non-committal and uninformative generalities. Don't say you are "the leading provider of innovative nutritional experiences in the fast-growing Ohio catering region."

- *Make sure the business model is clear.* One way to do this is to demonstrate clearly what on the site is free and what must be paid for. This sounds pretty obvious, but on many sites, it isn't clear. This is especially the case on media-related Web site. Visitors to magazine and newsletter Web sites often can't be sure what content is available at no charge and what must be paid for. I recall a site for a specialized financial services newsletter, which is available via subscription for about $1,400 annually. Yet the site publishes weekly headlines and articles that appear to be taken from the newsletter—at no charge to visitors. So I found myself wondering: Am I getting the $1,400 newsletter for free, some part of it, or something completely different? The site didn't make it clear, and since $1,400 is a lot to spend for a newsletter, I held off on ordering. Not the intended purpose, I am certain. And not a site to inspire investor confidence.

- *Provide supporting data.* In particular, you want to have as much in the way of endorsements from happy customers, or other information, which suggests there are significant numbers of satisfied buyers. An obvious approach is to quote from such customers. My use of written case histories was one way to communicate happy clients. If you have a restaurant or hotel, you might quote from written reviews. If you are a company that does large-scale projects, you might list the names of some of your clients.

The challenge for professional service companies tends to be getting clients to agree to be listed on your Web site. Some clients prefer not to have it known that they are using a particular kind of professional, and thus won't provide permission to be included on a company's Web site. It's up to you, then, to turn on the charm, or else disguise the case, or otherwise communicate the fact that you have satisfied customers.

- ***Provide some company lore and color.*** Be sure to provide some history about the company, like how it got started, what especially motivated the founders to settle on their product or service, and what makes the company's products and/or services superior to the competition. This is the place to provide the kind of background investors like to see that suggest a highly committed and motivated management team.

- ***Allow for ongoing communication with key constituencies.*** Investors are like anyone in your market in that they may or may not be ready to buy at the time they first visit your Web site. So you need to find ways to stay in touch with them. The best way to do that is via e-mail, such as a regular newsletter, or irregular updates.

  But how do you get visitors to want to sign up to stay in touch with you? Well, if they are buying something on your site, you can offer them the "opportunity" to receive information about future special events, new products, discounts, etc. Most will take you up on that opportunity. If you aren't actually selling something, then you need to be more creative and come up with something of real value. You may have to develop a newsletter with helpful hints that relate to your profession. Or you may have to provide ongoing news related to your industry. Remember, the idea here is to get visitors, including prospective investors, to share personal information about themselves.

  In addition to you feeding information to visitors, you should also try to find ways for them to feed you information—most notably, market research. It's become ever more easy to poll visitors to your site about how they feel about certain issues. For example, if you sell flowers via your site, you can poll visitors on flower attributes that are most important to them (freshness, free delivery, price, etc.), as well as asking them what they think about your products. Investors like to see you trying to obtain as much marketing data as possible.

What You Don't *Want from a Web Site*

There are a number of definite no-nos in putting together a Web site, things that will turn off investors faster than you can say, "What happened to the money?"

- *Making it difficult to navigate.* The emphasis should be on simplicity over all else. Pages should download quickly. The various sections of the site should be arranged logically, and be clearly labeled.
- *Leaving out important information.* One of the most irritating things business Web sites overlook is providing information on how to get in touch with key company officials. Failing to provide such information suggests you don't want to hear from customers or prospects. Yet some companies, especially technology companies, seem to go out of their way to make sure their Web sites are devoid of the names of company officials or of street addresses and phone numbers. This is a sure way to turn off investors, who want to see you reach out to your marketplace, not turn away from it.
- *Letting it become out of date.* A Web site that is out of date is like an Old West ghost town. It suggests that the best times are in the past, and that it's been abandoned for the future. The Web site updates shouldn't suddenly stop. The latest news releases shouldn't be six months or more old. Freshness counts for a lot on the Web.

And finally, what about competitive issues? How much do you reveal and how much hold back out of fear of revealing too much to competitors? This is a very difficult question to answer because there is no one right answer. If you are in a startup situation, you may be rightfully concerned about giving away too much about such things as your product's features or who your customers are. In that event, you may want to provide guidance to users to contact you for more information. That way you can question individuals who contact you about who they are and why they want the information. But be specific about the kind of information you are prepared to provide.

Putting It All Together

As I said at the start of this chapter, I don't want to reinvent the wheel in terms of providing advice about the basis of an effective Web site, since the Internet and bookstores are crammed with such information. I suggest you review some of this material.

Then, a key issue you face may be the task of making it happen. Do you purchase a software program or use an online service and do it yourself? Do you outsource everything?

Even though I spent several years running a business based on outsourcing Web matters, I'm inclined toward doing it yourself for an early-stage entrepreneur. While this may be more time consuming, it has two important advantages over outsourcing:

1.   It's much less costly. You can quickly run up large bills with an outsourcing company.
2.   It gives you flexibility and control to easily make changes.

The major exception to this advice is if you are developing a Web-dependent business with significant database and tool requirements. For example, if you are developing a real estate site with significant numbers of regularly changing home and apartment listings, you will need a substantial database and sophisticated tools to manage the listings and changes. Then, you may want to go the outsourcing route—though try to itemize costs, and be sure the outsourcing agency's tools are widely used so you can take control or easily switch to another provider. The goal is to be able to easily communicate with your market. ∎

Chapter 9

Use Publicity to Attract Investor Attention

CHAPTER SUMMARY

Media attention can be an effective technique for getting yourself noticed by investors, not to mention attracting customers. There are many ways of obtaining media exposure: ten are ranked in order of difficulty. Effective public relations requires constant attention. Here also is guidance on obtaining the professional help that fulfills your needs and fits your finances.

"Demonstrate why the market will accept your product or service in the context of the existing competitive landscape."
— *Venture capitalist participant in survey for this book*

I've been in the public relations business for more than 15 years, and in recent years, have seen ever more impressive examples of the power of publicity to influence investment decisions. Here are two examples, one of a client and another my own:

∾

A startup company that had just completed development of innovative software for the education market was referred to my agency in early 2001. The founder was beginning to make his company's product available to colleges and high schools on a trial basis for testing (i.e. for free). He was seeking to raise money from angel investors but, while he had raised a small amount, he hadn't yet received all the backing he needed. He concluded that public relations could help because media coverage conferred an important element of credibility. In a startup, credibility is one of the most difficult assets to come by.

Shortly after he signed on with my agency, his company was profiled in *The Boston Globe*. A few months after that, his company was profiled in *The New York Times*. Those and other "hits" encouraged new investor candidates to step forward, and convinced existing investor prospects who had been sitting on the sidelines to loosen up the purse strings. He raised the money he needed and, as a bonus, he also heard from several high schools and colleges that wanted to test his product; several of those inquiries led to sales.

&

Back in early 1999, my partner and I had decided that we wanted to sell our online marketing company, NetMarquee, which provided content and email services to major corporations, by the end of that year. Selling a company is akin to obtaining investment, since the acquirers of a business are using acquisition as an investment strategy to expand their own companies. But how could we alert prospective acquirers that we were for sale? We didn't want to just send out a business plan to the companies we thought should be interested in us.

We decided that the most impressive statement we could make to potential acquirers was that we had happy paying clients. And the best way to do that, we concluded, was to get some of our clients profiled in key industry trade publications. We targeted two of our clients and they agreed to be profiled, correctly assuming that publicity could help increase traffic to their Web sites.

Using our public relations expertise, we managed to get each client publicized in an important industry publication—one in an Internet weekly and the other in a direct marketing publication—with mention that NetMarquee was the agency responsible for their online success. The profiles became a key ingredient in leading three companies to make acquisition offers for NetMarquee, enabling us to select the most attractive overall package from among them, and sell the company in December 1999.

The Power of Publicity

Publicity, usually via media attention, is another way of sending the message to prospective investors that your company is achieving marketplace acceptance. Here are four things media attention can do for you vis-à-vis investors:

1. Alert prospective investors about your existence, so they investigate further. Investors are of the mindset that they need to find attractive investment candidates, rather than wait for the attractive investment candidates to find the investors. As just one example, a *Boston Globe* profile of venture firm TA Associates in June 2001, noted, "The firm keeps a database of nearly 200,000 companies—198,091 to be precise—that could one day become deal fodder…Names get added to the list as analysts comb through stories in hundreds of trade magazines and Sunday newspapers from major U.S. cities."

What happens if you get publicity and a venture capital firm calls and asks to see a copy of your business plan? Try this: Tell the representative you've been so busy filling orders and getting publicity that you haven't yet had a chance to complete your business plan, but that it's on your agenda, if you ever get a chance to catch your breath. That usually intrigues them even more, because they catch the scent of "fresh meat."

2.Provide ammunition that you can use to make available to targeted investors. If you have identified prospective investors, but haven't yet had serious discussions, or any discussions, then publicity can provide an excuse for getting in touch with them. This is essentially what my partner and I did when we were selling NetMarquee. We had in our research identified a handful of companies we thought would make appropriate acquirers. Once one of our clients was profiled in the Internet weekly, we picked up the phone, introduced ourselves to the candidates, and as part of an introductory package included the just-published article.

3. Reinforce any discussions you are having. To the extent that you are having serious discussions with investor candidates, publicity can help your cause. The educational software company I mentioned was in discussions with about a dozen prospective angel investors at the time the first profile, in *The Boston Globe*, came out. That helped make some on-again-off-again discussions on again. The reason isn't only credibility. When publicity comes out, serious prospective investors become nervous that they may lose their inside track to other investors who now learn about the company. They don't want to lose their fresh meat.

4. Attract customers. The right publicity is often a great way to stir up prospective customers or clients. Once you do that, of course, your overall story becomes that much better. As discussed in the next chapter, the more customers or customer prospects you have, the better your chances of attracting investment, and at improved terms.

Making Publicity Happen

All of the previous is nice, you might be saying, but how do I go about obtaining the kind of publicity that will win investment funds?

You need to satisfy two needs simultaneously:

1. Publicize things that will help your company.
2. Offer items of interest to the media.

Ideally, they're the same—you have a story to offer that helps your company attract customers and/or investors, and is also of interest to the media—but sometimes they aren't. You may want to focus on your great new product, while the media may see your product as a me-too ho-hum item that's already been covered elsewhere. Generally speaking, entrepreneurs focus much more on the first need, and much less on the second. By doing that, they limit their opportunities for media exposure, since to be successful it is necessary to focus as much or more on the second item. Savvy entrepreneurs think a lot about developing a "pitch" to the media that simultaneously satisfies both needs.

How do you best accomplish the two needs simultaneously? Here are several suggestions, from easiest to more difficult:

■ *Get yourself written up in your local community newspaper.* This is usually the easiest mission to accomplish, since most community newspapers are only too glad to publicize interesting local businesses. Try calling the editor and telling him or her that you recently started a new business in town producing an extremely innovative or interesting product or service that you think would be of interest to readers. This kind of publicity won't necessarily get you immediate customers, but if you live in a prosperous bedroom community where venture capitalists tend to live (such as Wellesley, MA, or Palo Alto, CA) it could help pique the curiosity of investors.

■ *Get yourself written up in an industry trade publication.* After your community newspaper, industry trade publications—the handful of weekly and monthly newspapers and magazines that cover particular industries—are usually the easiest to crack. The best way to receive attention is usually to issue a press release announcing your product or service. To improve the chances of the release being used, read the publications you are targeting first, so you know the approaches they take to announcing new products, and then try to mimic their articles. If different publications take different approaches, consider customizing your news release to match each publication's style.

Another way to attract the attention of industry trade publications is to offer the names of clients or customers using your services for the publications to profile. The media—especially the high-circulation trade publications—prefer case studies to writing about the

113

company producing a product or service. Editors tend to feel that their readers most prefer reading about products and services in action rather than simply publicizing companies trying to promote their products or services. The main challenge of using this technique is usually obtaining the permission of clients and customers to be profiled; they often prefer for competitive reasons to keep a low profile.

■ *Get written up in your local business publication.* Most large and mid-size cities now have a local business journal that comes out on a weekly basis. These publications are sometimes amenable to profiling new young companies. But if they're not, one effective way to get yourself highlighted is to write a column, often referred to as an "op ed" piece. These are opinion pieces, and usually the more provocative they are, the better chance they have of being published. An op-ed may have to do with a particular trend in your industry that is having special ramifications. For example, if your company produces an environmentally-related product, you may be in a position to write credibly about some aspect of pollution or global warming. Generally speaking, you want to avoid being overly self-promotional in such articles, focusing instead on establishing yourself as a credible spokesperson; your brief bio at the end of the column is the part that will steer prospective customers and/or investors your way.

■ *Get written up in your metropolitan paper.* This is more difficult to accomplish than the previous types of outlets, but it can be done, with the right approach. Metropolitan papers like *The Boston Globe, Dallas Morning News,* and *San Francisco Chronicle* are interested in exciting local companies, it's just that the competition for space is more fierce than in community and trade publications. One of the best ways to attract the attention of editors is to package your company's founder or president or top technologist as someone who is especially interesting, exciting, innovative, creative, or otherwise is an unusual personality. This takes a special kind of pitching, but such stories can go a long way toward attracting prospective customers and/or investors.

●□*Gain attention in a national business publication.* Getting yourself written up in something like *The Wall Street Journal, Business Week,* or *Fortune* is the most difficult media challenge around. These publications are inundated with business owners who want to be mentioned, and most pitches wind up in the round file. It is possible to crack these publications, though, and one of the best techniques is to conduct some kind of industry survey that the publications can report on. This may be a survey of prospective customers or prospects about how their attitudes toward a particularly timely issue or problem. For example, after the September 11 terror attacks, the national business media were especially interested in surveys about how consumers and businesses were changing their travel habits; if your company was involved somehow with the travel industry, such a survey could have attracted you media attention. The keys to successfully getting a survey noticed by the media are, first, to be sure to sample enough respondents—typically a couple hundred or more—and to keep the questions focused on areas of interest to businesspeople or consumers and make them non-self-promotional. With surveys easier than ever to carry out via the Internet and email, this is an increasingly attractive publicity option. Just one note of caution: Be careful about doing surveys in the area of health care, since editors and reporters are especially enamored of scientific studies carried out by universities and nonprofit organizations, and biased against studies carried out by individual companies.

115

Leverage Your Success

What should you expect from the publicity you receive? As a public relations professional, I consistently find that this is one of the toughest questions to answer. I have seen clients get written up extensively in *The Wall Street Journal* and wind up with little or no reaction. And I've seen clients with a small mention in a community or trade publication receive significant customer orders.

Regardless of what directly happens from a mention in the media, there are things you can do to leverage the positive impact of a media placement:

- *Let prospective investors know about the media attention.* If you have been in touch with venture capitalists, send them a copy of the article, or an email with a link to the article.
- *Include the article as part of any background information you send out in the future to prospective investors.* Positive media attention gives you credibility that you should take advantage of.
- *Use the article as a means to obtain additional media attention.* Articles that mention your company can sometimes be used to influence editors at non-competing publications to write about you. For example, a write up of your product or service in a trade publication may help persuade a reporter with a metropolitan daily, or even a national business publication heavily read by investors, to explore writing you up.

You may receive some calls from prospective customers and/or investors. Then again, you may see very little activity. In any event, you should keep tabs of all the publicity, reproduce articles that mention you on nice paper and in color, if appropriate, and use the clippings in as many ways as possible to further your cause.

116

How Should You Handle the PR Function Ongoing?

One thing I don't want to convey here is that public relations is a one-time event—a matter of getting a single product announcement or op-ed piece published. Public relations can be a very effective means of letting prospective investors know not only about your existence, but about your ongoing progress and growth—if it is exploited on a consistent ongoing basis.

For public relations to be exploited to its fullest by entrepreneurs requires a significant investment in time, energy, and sometimes money. If you agree with what I have said here, then a key decision you have to make is whether to handle public relations internally with your own people or externally by hiring an agency.

Because I've been in the agency business for many years, my prejudice is toward engaging an agency. Then you don't have to worry about learning how to write a press release, obtaining the names of media outlets and, most important, doing the followup work that is key to getting the media to write about you.

Fine, you say, but how does a young business like mine pay the monthly $5,000 and up it costs for an agency? It's difficult, and may not be viable if you are operating in a very cash-short situation. Here are a couple of possible ways around this challenge:

1. Hire a freelance PR specialist who has contacts in the media to help you in pitching and followup. The media are used to hearing from PR people, so it doesn't hurt your company. And chances are the hourly fees will be lower, and you can control the hours expended more tightly than you might with an agency.

2. Work out an equity arrangement with a public relations agency. Some agencies will take some or all of their fees in company stock or stock options. I have done that in a few special circumstances where I was especially impressed by a young company and its management team.

3. The bottom line here is that you should obtain as much exposure as possible for your company. Positive media attention helps you look more established than you might otherwise, and helps foster an image of success among prospective investors. ■

Chapter 10

Touch the Marketplace

CHAPTER SUMMARY

The most convincing evidence you can provide to investors of your company's potential is actual sales or orders. Here are ten ways to demonstrate demand for your product or service that will impress investors. Next, publicize your success stories to make it easier for investors to commit.

"Customer acceptance is the most important factor. There are lots of great solutions out there looking for problems to solve."
                                    —*Venture capitalist participant in survey for this book*

M ichael J. (not his real name) is a recent graduate of a well regarded East Coast college that specializes in training its undergraduates in various business topics. Michael focused on entrepreneurship. When the college set up a business incubator—essentially free office space, computers, and other amenities for qualifying businesses in exchange for stock—Michael jumped at the chance. He saw an opening to leave his less-than-satisfying job and launch a specialty Internet-based business.

Michael's first task? Write a business plan. This was what he had been taught in his entrepreneurship courses at the college. Week after week, Michael sat at his desk in the basement of a college administration building where the incubator was based, and wrote the business plan for his dream—an online Asian-American portal. He wrote the business plan, and then he re-wrote the plan, and then he re-wrote it again. It would be his ticket to raising the several hundred thousand dollars of investment funds he had determined he needed to launch the business. After several rewrites, the business plan actually read very smoothly.

In the process of doing market research for his plan, he had spoken with proprietors of laundromats in Asian neighborhoods of Boston about the possibility of them making the portal available to their customers via on-site computers they would install. They were receptive to the idea of creating a new device for attracting customers and keeping them engaged while they dropped quarters into the washers and dryers.

But Michael neglected to even include this important marketing-sales information in his business plan. No investors ever put money into Michael's business. While I can't say for sure why they didn't, it seems clear that one significant reason was that he offered little hard evidence that the business he envisioned so beautifully in the business plan would actually obtain customers and operate profitably. So he gave up and went back to a job.

I have disguised the exact circumstances because I was a "mentor" to Michael, at the behest of college faculty members. I don't want to violate confidences, nor do I want to embarrass the college, which was merely doing what hundreds of other colleges do in emphasizing the preparation of a business plan in their courses on entrepreneurship.

What was especially striking to me in my experience mentoring Michael was that he seemed unable to follow through on firming up deals with some of the prospective customers he had spoken with as part of the marketing research for his business plan. You can have the most beautifully written business plan in the world, but investors are much more turned on by evidence of customers, I told him. Re-visit some of those laundromat proprietors and try to obtain letters of intent or perhaps even formal agreements. Then you'll have something substantive to show investors as evidence that you can sell your product.

But my advice seemed foreign to Michael. He had learned his business plan lessons so well, he couldn't be moved. And following those lessons so scrupulously cost him a chance at starting a potentially lucrative business.

Why Demonstrating Demand Is So Important

I discussed in Chapter 4 how closely investors examine the entrepreneurs, and try to assess their mindsets and skills. As part of this examination process, though, they want evidence that the entrepreneurs can actually bring in business on the projected scale. The emphasis here is on "evidence." You may not be able to produce sales on the projected scale until you have investment funds—to complete development, acquire materials, or assemble the manufacturing facilities. But you can show evidence, and the stronger the evidence, the better chance you have of succeeding on two fronts:

1. Actually raising the money you are looking for;
2. Raising it on better terms than you would otherwise.

Ten Ways to Demonstrate Demand

So the challenge here is simple: How do you demonstrate as concretely as possible that the marketplace you have targeted will actually purchase your product or service? The key to answering this question for your business is to assess all the possible ways to show customer interest.

This can be a chicken-and-egg kind of situation. You may not have your product well enough developed that you can offer it for sale. Yet you need to figure out a way to convince prospective customers to show interest in it. Here are ten ways to demonstrate marketplace interest, from the most desirable to the least desirable.

1. ***Take advance orders.*** Just because you don't have a
   product or service ready for prime time, there's
   nothing that says you can't take advance orders. The
   key here is not only to have a product or service that
   prospects are drooling over, but to be prepared to
   commit to delivering it by a certain date. Failure to
   meet the deadline could cost you orders, and more
   importantly, customer goodwill. Unhappy customers
   or prospects have a way of spreading the word
   around an industry much more quickly than do
   satisfied customers.

2. ***Obtain a letter of intent.*** This is similar to obtaining
   an advance order, just a bit more tentative.
   Essentially, it commits a prospect to buying a product
   if certain conditions are met, such as deadlines,
   features, and quality. But prospective investors
   understand that a letter of intent usually has enough
   escape clauses that even if a young company meets
   its end of the bargain, a prospective customer may in
   the end fail to follow through with the actual
   purchase. You can beef up the effectiveness of a
   letter of intent by obtaining a deposit, even if it's
   refundable; money speaks louder than words.
   Generally speaking, prospective investors know that
   the briefer the time horizon of a letter of intent, the
   likelier the customer is to actually follow through.

3. ***Build a pipeline.*** To the extent that you solicit
   prospective customers and get them to talk to you
   about potentially buying your product, you are
   assembling what is known in sales circles as a
   "pipeline"—a list of prospective buyers. Being able
   to list these prospects in your presentation and
   synopsis—ideally with some sort of rating about the
   seriousness of their interest—tells potential investors
   that you take the sales process seriously. They know

that most of the prospects in your pipeline probably won't pan out, but they'll admire you for beginning the process. One of the questions you'll be asked by investors is what percentage of your pipeline can be expected to turn into real customers—a question you won't be able to answer with confidence until you've been in business a while.

4. *Obtain a letter of interest.* This is just what it suggests—a written expression of interest by a prospective customer, usually based on a request you make to help you document to prospective investors that there is marketplace interest. It is the next step down in the hierarchy of written commitments. It is important because it shows more than casual interest by prospective buyers, but it conveys nothing even bordering on a legal commitment. If you assemble enough of them—say three or four for an expensive product—then the letters can impress prospective investors.

5. *Show Web site inquiries.* If you have a Web site designed to demonstrate customer actions, you have potential evidence of marketplace interest. For example, you may be able to provide numbers and lists of Web site visitors who requested product information. Or you may have numbers and lists of individuals who signed up to be kept informed about product developments. To the extent that the numbers are increasing over a period of time, then you have something potentially credible. Simple Web site traffic statistics—like number of page views— usually isn't as credible as some kind of online action.

6. *Develop a survey.* This is the old-fashioned kind of market research. You develop a survey asking prospective users about their likely interest in your

product or service. The higher the numbers of individuals surveyed and the more positive the results, the more convincing the survey is to prospective investors. One of the key challenges is locating prospective customers and getting them to participate—the process can be very time-consuming and expensive if you survey individuals by phone or snail mail. The Internet has eased the problems associated conducting surveys via use of email solicitation and online forms. If you have an email list of prospective customers, you can use an online survey service to send them emails and direct them to an online questionnaire. The process is obviously much less costly and time-consuming than the traditional way.

7. *Collect inquiries at a trade show.* An efficient way to collect the names of prospective customers is to demonstrate your product or service at an industry trade show. You set up a booth and obtain the business cards of everyone who has an interest in what you are selling. Demonstrating at a trade show, of course, assumes you have something to demonstrate. It also assumes you have the cash for the often substantial costs associated with exhibiting—booth rental, display construction, travel, and various other expenses—that can total several thousand dollars. And while you collect names via business cards or signup sheets, you tend not to know the seriousness of many of the prospects, except for those you are able to speak with at length and who say they are seriously interested.

8. *Solicit advertising inquiry cards.* Related to the previous technique is that of placing advertisements that invite a customer response card. Typically such advertisements are placed in industry trade

publications. Your ad introduces your product or service, and urges readers to fill out a magazine inquiry card, with your company's product number circled. The people who send in inquiries can be considered prospects for you to call on and offer additional information. A variation is to advertise on the radio or in newspapers, and invite inquiries via an 800 or 888 call-in line. Like trade shows, advertisements are expensive, typically running several thousand dollars each. And you usually need to place several ads to obtain a significant enough response to make the process worthwhile. Ideally, you should follow up with each one to be able to classify the degree of real interest these prospects have.

9. ***Obtain speaking engagements.*** Giving a talk in front of a group of prospective customers can be an effective way to obtain the names of the most seriously interested prospects. The challenge is to get yourself invited to speak before an appropriate group. You may be able to do it through a local chamber of commerce, or an industry trade group. Many of these organizations arrange for speakers months in advance, and often insist on individuals who have a proven record of effective public speaking and who won't promote themselves. Still and all, it sometimes is possible for a startup or early-stage entrepreneur to get himself or herself invited to be a member of a panel or the head of a discussion group. At these sessions, you will likely want to make your talk informational, but if you skillfully handle the presentation, you should be able to weave in something about your company's product or service.

10. ***Seek out "love letters."*** The last approach I'll offer is an old favorite of mine. So-called "love letters,"

whereby individuals who have sampled your product or service write you with their comments, can be an effective tool in turning investors' heads. Unless these letters come from real-life customers, though, they may lose some of their credibility. Someone who writes a letter saying how much they admire your product sample or service demonstration still hasn't passed the ultimate test that investors demand—shown that they'll make a purchase at a particular price.

Turning Investors' Heads

The ten steps just described are a sampling of techniques for supplying ammunition to your market and revenue projections. You may be able to think of other approaches for divining prospect lists that will make an impression on investors. Beyond such techniques are a few other managerial sorts of things you can do to impress investors that you are serious about aggressively seeking out business:

- *Hire a rainmaker.* Investors love to see entrepreneurs building up sales teams that include individuals with proven records of generating substantial sales. So-called rainmakers are those especially talented individuals who are able to produce significant sales within a product or service area. Every successful company has one or more such individuals, and investors know how key they are to long-term success. Thus, if you can attract such an individual early on, you will do a lot to impress investors.

- *Publicize your sales successes.* Every time you actually make a sale, or bring in a beta test site, you should get the word out about your accomplishment. Your bragging may only take the form of an email to

126

prospective investors. But it may also take the form of a news release to the media. Success breeds success, so to the extent your initial customers don't object, you should let the world know what you have accomplished.

- ***Monitor your customers' reactions.*** Investors also like to see that you are keeping tabs on customers— on what they like and dislike about your product or service. The information you collect about how customers are using a sample or beta product can provide important insights into the features and benefits you should stress for the future.

In today's high-stress investment environment, sales are what it is all about for investors. You can't afford to be bashful in finding ways to locate prospective buyers, and get your product or service into their hands. ■

Part III

Business Planning and the Investment Process

At this point, you've done all the leg work. You've developed a presentation, a synopsis, and a Web site. You've made some sales, or have identified customers ready to order, and you've obtained some publicity. You may even have investors checking you out. What do you do next?

You may or may not need to prepare a formal business plan now. The chapters in this third section explore the process of locating and negotiating for investment funds. They examine the underlying dynamics of entrepreneur-investor psychology, along with a number of possible scenarios in negotiating with investors, including a first-person case study involving an entrepreneur who attracted financing from AOL. There is also guidance on networking, investor conferences, and other such issues around locating money, along with the realities of valuation and dilution.

As you read through these chapters, you'll appreciate why there is much more to actually obtaining investment funds than a business plan.

Chapter 11

What You're Selling and What Investors Are Buying
Capitalize on Investor Psychology

CHAPTER SUMMARY
It's essential that entrepreneurs understand investor psychology, and discard the many misconceptions that exist about investor expertise and expectations. Sometimes investors behave like a herd of cattle and sometimes they get greedy. The key to negotiating effectively is having convincing evidence to develop a realistic valuation for your company. Here are ways to potentially increase your company's valuation, and the likelihood that you'll retain control.

"If you get an audience with investors, they will probably give you feedback that you should consider in determining a business strategy. Listen to what they tell you."

—*Venture capitalist participant in survey for this book*

C onsider the following situations, and how you might react:

You're in the market to buy a house in a suburb with a market so tight that bidding wars sometimes erupt over especially desirable homes. It's a Saturday afternoon and you have just enough time to look at one house. Your real estate broker says he has two possibilities: he can get you a sneak preview of one that is just about to come on the market the next day, or you can look at another one that has all the features you are seeking, but for unknown reasons has been on the market for a month.

❧

You're looking for a used Toyota Camry. You're under the gun because your own 12-year-old car's transmission has just given out, among other problems. A friend tells you his 75-year-old grandmother is about to trade in her three-year-old Toyota Camry, with 18,000 miles, for a new one, but would be willing to sell it. There's also a Toyota Camry with about the same features and mileage that you saw on a dealer's lot a week earlier; the dealer has already followed up with three phone calls to see if you'll buy it.

❧

You're the manager of sales at a radio station. Your best sales woman has just left, and you need someone quickly who can come in and be productive. A colleague tells you about a young woman who's been going gangbusters selling newspaper advertising for a local paper, but who would love to get into radio. You also have in front of you the resume of a man you've never met but who's sold advertising for a number of radio stations, and has left each of his previous four jobs after 12 to 18 months.

If you're like most people, you'd go after the first rather than the second option in each situation described. You'd want a shot at the house no one else has yet seen before you look at the one that's been languishing on the market. You'd prefer the "cream puff" car from someone you know to the one sitting on a used car lot. And you'd rather have the hot-shot sales person than the journeyman.

Now imagine you are the head of a venture capital firm that specializes in investing in companies making advanced materials. An accountant calls to tell you about this neat little startup that has developed a new material that can be used to make the rocks used in gas grills generate twice their usual heat, and thus cook meats and fish much more

132

quickly. The company has made a few small sales to grill manufacturers that are testing it out.

"Have them send me a business plan," you tell the accountant.

"They don't have a business plan," the accountant replies. "They've been too busy perfecting the product and getting their first customers. But they need financing to prepare themselves for the fast growth that now looks very likely over the next year. They're going to approach a few venture firms, but I told them you'd be a great match for them because of your expertise in the materials area. Can you arrange to meet them in the next day or two?"

You look over at the pile of business plans on a corner of your desk that have come in unsolicited, many of them promising various sorts of exotic and revolutionary materials. You had planned to read through them during some free time you have over the next day or two.

Where would you likely spend that upcoming free time? On the "fresh meat" that no one else has yet had a look at, or the pile of business plans, many of them likely heavily shopped among other venture capitalists?

Do you think you would be turned off because the company recommended by your accountant friend doesn't have a business plan? Let's put it this way: Isn't it possible that the fact it doesn't have a business plan might be a turn-on? After all, it's being recommended by someone you know and trust. You have a chance to get in first, before other "buyers." It's a little like that house about to come on the market. Who cares that the promotional paperwork hasn't been completed quite yet?

And indeed, the venture capitalists I sampled confirm this hypothesis. Some 40 of the 42 venture capitalists in my survey said the most highly desirable investment candidates are "referred to me by someone whose judgment I trust—a colleague, professional, friend, etc." And as I noted previously, 41 of the 42 said they would be willing to meet with intriguing entrepreneurs, even if they don't have a business plan.

Human Nature

Let me just say at this point that there isn't one way to approach venture capitalists and other investors, any more than there is one way to sell a car or a house. And in that respect, entrepreneurs have been seriously misled in recent years. The media propaganda machines have created the "rule" that you can't approach professional investors without a completed business plan. Yet I know venture capitalists who have invested in situations where there's not only not a business plan, but not even a real business. This occurs most commonly when venture capitalists put up money to help an academic with a potentially significant technology assemble a company. It also happens when they fund an entrepreneur with a track record of building one or more previously successful companies before he or she has even fully formed a new company. Or one who is especially articulate and charismatic to the point that he or she can articulate the business concept in especially convincing terms.

Aside from the misconceptions entrepreneurs have about the role of the business plan, there are also misconceptions about the role of investors. There's a tendency to think that venture capitalists and other professional investors are super sophisticated financial gurus who apply complex strategic models to select which business plans to fund. But they're just people. Sure, they're professionals, but they get greedy. They're subject to the herd instinct. They're always on the lookout for a good deal.

Just look at what happened to many of them during the mid and late 1990s dot-com craze. By the early 2000s, some dozens were out of the venture business entirely, while many others were still licking their wounds, and will be for many years based on the greed and herd mentality that overtook the industry. One such example is Bill Gross, founder of something called Idealab, a privately held

California "incubator" that provided money, people, and space for new ventures. Idealab funded more than a dozen Internet companies. One of its guiding principles was that it wouldn't invest more than $250,000 in a venture based on the premise that if a company couldn't attract venture capital funds beyond that amount when the time of need arose, it possibly didn't deserve to survive. Yet Gross became so enamored of one of Idealab's companies that he violated his own rule and pumped more than $800,000 into it—before it failed. And that became just the first of numerous instances in which greed drove Gross to violate his own rule.

In March 2001, Gross wound up pictured on the cover of *Fortune*, accompanied by the heading: "I lost $800 million in eight months. Why am I still smiling?" Investors sued Idealab in an effort to recover losses.

Gross had let greed cloud his professional judgment, and it cost him dearly. And he was just one of many, though one of only a very few willing to go public with his sad tale. One venture capitalist quoted in the March 2002 issue of *Upside* magazine predicted that 200 to 300 of the 800 members of the National Venture Capital Association (NVCA), will disappear before long.

The point here is that the investment process isn't the formal rigid process the consultants and academics might have us think. Rather, it's not unlike many of the substantial investment decisions many of us make at different times in our lives—buying a car or a house, or hiring a key sales person. We try to discover good deals and reduce our risk by obtaining recommendations and inside information, and avoiding buying with the crowds. And sometimes we get sucked into going with the crowd, and making big mistakes.

Investor Secrets

Venture capitalists are a little like insurance salespeople. They like to maintain an aura of mystery and confusion about what they do, and for very good reason. Sellers of life insurance don't want prospective customers to fully appreciate what a poor investment traditional whole life insurance really is, so the sales people intentionally talk in mumbo jumbo about "maturities" and "double indemnity." Then they make sure to talk about "protecting your family" and "what if something happens to you as the breadwinner"—all as part of a carefully choreographed effort to create insecurity and fear.

So it is with venture capitalists and other professional investors. They speak before groups of entrepreneurs and talk about the importance of writing a good business plan. Their real goal, though, is to spread the word about themselves so that one or another contact will alert them to the next Microsoft or Dell Computer before contacting someone else.

This point was driven home to me by a profile of TA Associates, one of the nation's premier venture capital firms, in *The Boston Globe* in June 2001, which I alluded to in Chapter 10. The article described how TA Associates systematically seeks out investment candidates, to the extent that it has a database of nearly 200,000 companies "that could one day become deal fodder." According to the article, the firm's chief executive "says the ground-floor method of finding good investments brings deal flow that rivals don't find if they rely only on investment bankers, lenders, and luck for opportunities."

The key word in this analysis is "deal flow." Investors want to see the best possible investment candidates for their firms before their competitors see them. To do that, they have to be out hustling. The whole thrust of TA's efforts is to find investment candidates. There was no mention in the article about TA's process for reviewing business plans being sent in over the transom, but I guarantee you they receive little or no attention.

The Bottom Line

There's more to the whole investment process than simply reducing risk. When you obtain inside information about a new house, car, or employee, your ultimate goal is to get the best possible deal on your investment. You're hoping that because you've obtained an inside track, you can avoid competitive bidding, and can therefore get a great deal.

And that's the way it is with professional investors. They want to find the best possible investment candidates and then negotiate the largest possible stake in them at the lowest possible investment price.

Entrepreneurs often don't fully appreciate this part of the entire process. In my experience, they're just so anxious to obtain funds that entrepreneurs don't think about what the funds might cost them in ownership—until it's too late. Nor do they think about what they can do to move the pendulum in their favor.

Dilution and the Economics of Investing

You may be wondering, what does all this explanation have to do with the business plan? Everything. To fully appreciate the relationship, you need to understand the economics of investing. Essentially, it goes like this:

The most important single step in the investment process is placing a value on your company. Everything else regarding the investment decision-making process emanates from this step. Here's a hypothetical situation to explain what I mean:

Let's say you get a group of investors interested in your company, and they decide that your company has a value of $1 million.

Now let's say you are seeking $500,000 of investment funds.

That means that $500,000 buys half the company— that you would have to give up half your company to get the $500,000.

But now let's say that the same investor group determines that the value is $2 million. This has huge implications, because at a $2 million valuation, the same $500,000 only buys one-fourth of the company. You'd only have to give up 25% of your company to get the same money.

Welcome to the concept of dilution. Most basically, each time you accept investment funds in exchange for stock in your company, you reduce your own holdings. The concept is well illustrated by capitalization and dilution tables, examples of which have been put together by Michael Gonnerman, the financial expert quoted in Chapter 7, and are available at www.gonnerman.com.

Valuations that investors arrive at are to some degree arbitrary. But they are also grounded in marketplace realities—factors like what other companies in your industry are being valued at, the amount of current sales you are generating, expected future growth, and the expertise of your management team. You don't have control over all these factors—most particularly what other companies in your industry are being valued at—but you do have control over many of them. For example, as described in Chapter 10, you may be able to begin selling your product, and thus show current sales.

The key challenge facing you as an entrepreneur is to figure out how to increase the value of your company as much as possible before you go looking for investment funds. Accomplishing that is a much different task than simply preparing a business plan.

The Proper Reaction to Investor Interest

How does all this come into play in real life? Consider this situation:

I was consulting to a startup business that involved a new kind of consumer finance technique. The key issue involved the entrepreneur's approach to raising money. He was initially looking for a few hundred thousand dollars to test out the concept. He approached a group of investors he was introduced to by a mutual acquaintance.

The response was what you might expect. "Send us a business plan."

So the entrepreneur decided he'd need to stop everything and spend several weeks, minimum, preparing a business plan. I advised him to consider another approach: Use the upcoming several weeks to do other things—develop a presentation, build a Web site, and try to obtain some initial commitments from his target market to use the eventual product. Based on those steps, he could easily write a two-page summary of his concept.

Then, he could call those investors or others and tell them that he was still "in the process" of preparing his business plan, but hadn't been able to complete it because of all the great things happening in the business. He'd send along a written summary of the business concept, but he'd need to meet them personally to communicate all the great things that were happening.

When he met them, he'd be in a much stronger negotiating position than if he'd just spent all his time writing a plan. He took the advice and eventually pocketed several hundred thousand dollars of investment funds that he then applied to further proving the concept.

The fact of the matter is that the professional investment community is going through its own mammoth changes. Here's how Jeffry Timmons of Babson explains it:

"In my view, the old investing model demanded a nearly complete jig-saw puzzle. Unless the entrepreneur could show via the business plan, track record, strategy and team that *at least 90%* or more of the pieces of the jig-saw puzzle were in place, *and* unless the investors could quickly *conclude*: I see exactly what is missing; I know who and/or where to obtain those pieces; they are very affordable; and I can do it soon enough; the investors would reject the deal. Only when the jig-saw puzzle was 90-95% complete would a term sheet for a proposed deal be on the table. Such an approach by investors today, while prevalent, is facing serious obsolescence."

The point here is that you don't have to comply with the knee-jerk reaction from prospective investors to produce a business plan that shows how you've worked everything out. Yes, at some point you may have to show a plan to financial backers, but it won't be the only reason, or likely even the main reason, you get your money. Rather, it will be a supporting document, much like a resume.

Your challenge is to increase the value of your company, and show investors how their funds will further increase the value of your company. ■

Chapter 12

Teaming Up with AOL for Love and Money: A Case Study

CHAPTER SUMMARY

This tale of how one entrepreneur raised more than $50 million illustrates many of the points raised earlier in this book. The most effective tools at this entrepreneur's disposal were: an effective presentation, an impressive Web site, great karma, existing customers and partners, and an effective public relations strategy that maximized his company's visibility. Also key: a network of significant contacts.

"Expect to be grilled. Experienced investors have seen lots of plans. They have been in lots of deals and know probably better than you all that can go wrong. They've earned their cynicism, even if they won't show you their scars."
—Venture capitalist participant in survey for this book

A among the new realities of raising investment funds in the late 1990s and early 2000s is that it is no longer a one-time or two-time special event, but rather an ongoing process—or headache. Moreover, financing doesn't necessarily come from one of the hundreds of venture capital firms; it can also come from a large (and well-fortified) corporation in the form of a strategic alliance that can vary widely in form and resources provided. Equally significant, the process whereby financing is completed is far from rigid and well defined.

Smaller growing companies that understand how the financing landscape has changed have been well rewarded with essential resources like cash and marketing muscle from major corporations like Yahoo!, Microsoft, IBM, AOL Time Warner, and others, in exchange for a key technology, essential content, or some other perceived "missing link" in the corporate offerings. In some cases, the partnerships have provided the credibility young companies need to grow further and prove their concept enough that venture capitalists will finally invest in them. In others, they have led to attractive acquisition offers down the road.

But how does an unknown and under-financed early-stage business become the focus of a cash-rich corporation? Certainly for such an important arrangement, you'd need a carefully crafted written business plan, right? Wrong.

Developing a Partnership with AOL

For a number of years in the early and mid-1990s, I argued forcefully in talks I gave to entrepreneur groups that one of the best uses of a written business plan was to attract a potential corporate strategic partner. A business plan, I reasoned, gives you the credibility that large corporations prefer, since it suggests that you are as savvy and sophisticated about planning as they are, or at least as they are supposed to be.

While that may have been the case some years ago, it is a long way from the evolving reality of entrepreneurial life in the late 1990s and into the new century. An entrepreneur friend of mine, Jonathan Carson, spent much of the 1990s starting and building a company known as Family Education Network, which developed and disseminated education-related content to parents of school-age children—first via paper newsletters and later via a sophisticated Web site. I followed Jon's exploits on a blow-by-blow basis because I was an early investor in his venture.

For him, obtaining essential financing was a constant headache, even during the heady financing days of the mid and late 1990s, partly because education wasn't seen by many investors as an attractive growth area. So he turned eventually to an alliance with one of the most influential corporations of the time—America Online.

He had co-founded Family Education Network in 1990, during the depths of a previous recession, and by 1997 had turned it into the leading Internet company in the emerging area of parent education information, with a growing network of local school Web sites built on FEN's hosting platform. It positioned itself as the key link between the nation's public schools and parents.

Jon is an expert communicator and, based on my involvement, he and I developed this first-person account of his company's challenge, and its unfolding relationship with AOL. You can determine for yourself the key components of his aggressive and dramatic effort to link up with a major corporation in the story that follows.

A Marketing and Financing Conundrum—An Entrepreneur's Tale

Even though education was the second-largest single market behind health care, companies like FEN still represented a nascent area, and investors in particular had yet to recognize our legitimacy. To them, we looked like some kind of nonprofit organization because of our close links to education organizations like the PTA. But we knew the market was huge. Our space had 40 million parents of school-age children, 40 million school-age kids, and 5 million educators. K-12 is a $300 billion industry. All together just under a third of the country is directly involved in the education of kids.

Three years after our launch, in 1993, I had convinced a deep-pocketed Asian investor to back us. He is a billionaire and billionaires generally make big bets. My pitch was that if we built THE trusted and credible franchise in education, this would be very valuable in the 21st century to the public markets or to a potential acquirer. So beginning in 1993, he and a small venture capital firm invested $300,000 into FEN in return for approximately 15% of the company.

I envisioned a very enticing model—one based on the American Association of Retired Persons (AARP). AARP was an $11 billion organization that served a generation of seniors by offering insurance and other products and services at special discounts, as well as conducting legislative advocacy. I thought this same model could be applied to education by serving the caretakers for kids—parents and teachers. One of our important cheerleaders early on was former Sen. Paul Tsongas, who became a member of our board and ran for President in '92. Once I fully understood the enormous power of AARP, the idea of an 'AARP for parents, teachers, and kids' met my requirements of being simultaneously big, meaningful, and socially responsible.

But it was unclear how we were actually going to build a big-business model. AARP had developed a killer insurance product for seniors. We had started by selling newsletter and seminar programs to large corporations that supported working parents, known as work/family programs. The problem was that work/family programs are generally purchased by human resource departments, which are referred to in corporate speak as 'cost centers' (e.g. they represent only cost to the corporation, no revenue). After the Gulf War of 1990-91, cost centers became increasingly risky places to sell to, as corporate America began the ongoing effort of downsizing and squeezing costs. So while we were achieving success and adding big clients like Merck, AT&T, IBM and others, I knew this was not going to be the big business I envisioned. Put another way, this was not AARP for kids. But it was building credibility as a provider of education content to parents.

Fortunately, our Asian investor continued to support us by writing checks as we added a few more employees and looked into various opportunities. By late 1996, we were the first significant education Web site, www.familyeducation.com, and had strategic partnerships with all the big education grass roots groups like National PTA. We had a staff of over 30 engineers and content producers, and were consuming over $200,000 a month. But I had not been able to bring in any new investors to take the load off our Asian investor. Education was seen as a difficult market that had confounded others in the past, though educational software had raised awareness of parents' insatiable demand for technology solutions to learning.

As 1996 turned into 1997, our Asian investor was gradually losing patience. There was an Asian financial crisis, and his investment in FEN was now over $7 million and growing monthly, with no end in sight. To use a venture capital term, he was becoming 'tired,' and wanted to either seen another investor validate his bet or see revenues rise fast enough to offset the need for investment. We were struggling to find either. This led to a Catch 22: Without momentum, it was hard to bring in capital. But without capital, it was difficult to attract the management talent we needed to establish momentum.

Making a Key Contact

In the spring of 1997, with cash running short, one of our board members learned from a contact of his that AOL was looking seriously at the education market, and was in scarch of a vehicle to enter the market. A fellow named Miles Gilburne was leading the initiative, and my board member and the contact agreed that it made sense for Miles and me to talk. I went digging for background on Miles to see where he stood in the AOL hierarchy, and what I found out made me do a double take. Miles was one of the top ten executives at AOL, and its top dealmaker. Just to put this in perspective, an entrepreneur's biggest challenge in getting a partnership deal with a major corporation completed is getting to the right guy. And by the looks of it, we had found him on our first try.

My initial phone conversation with Miles took place at noon on May 3 and lasted less than 10 minutes, during which time I gave what had become my usual pitch, honed through countless investor presentations—my vision for how to capture leadership in the education category of the Internet. FEN would effect real change in the education system by building a highly endorsed, highly credible online education portal that delivered services for parents that would be both a commerce hub and a platform for "demand-side" parent-driven education reform. In essence, our message was that it was the parents, stupid. They had the money, they had the need, and as many parent board members reminded me, they had the guilt. The brief call ended with Miles suggesting that he come up to Boston and pay me a visit. Lock and load, Houston, we had a live one.

The Introductory Pitch

Ten days after that phone call, Miles was in Boston to listen to the full pitch. Unbeknownst to me, Miles had come up to Boston the prior evening and had dinner with an old pal of his at Softbank, one of the most aggressive investors in Internet companies. Earlier in the year, we had met this individual and tried to convince Softbank to invest. He had liked the idea and had become a big champion of ours within Softbank. But investment discussions had ultimately stalled over the item that many such discussions stall over—stock price. We thought our stock should be accorded a higher value than Softbank did. The discussions ended amicably, though, with all sorts of talk about maybe getting together again in the near future. Given this individual's enthusiasm for us, it was likely that Miles got timely and important validation that he had found the right company to work with in K-12 education.

As I walked out to the reception area the morning of May 14th, I was a little surprised at what I saw. Here was a tall gangly guy with a beard dressed in blue jeans who could have passed for an older graduate student or a latter day Vermont hippie. "Hmm," I remember thinking, "this is different." Admittedly by 1997 the work dress code was in full retreat but one did not typically find officers of major companies like AOL dressed in jeans.

As we settled down to talk, a few things struck me. First was that he seemed personally interested in education. On several occasions he said he thought education was the most important activity that society can engage in. And he said it in a way that I believed. By then I had seen a lot of phonies who had clearly never thought about kids or school since they were in one. But Miles seemed the real McCoy. Second, he was a top-down strategic thinker. Top down thinkers start at a very conceptually strategic level and drill down to particulars, but generally don't spend much time on the details, figuring that they will change as the business evolves. I like to think of myself as being in the same mode. I was taken.

In small-group situations, I generally introduced FEN via a PowerPoint slide presentation. In this type of one-on-one situation, though, I want the other person to have a chance to size me up and I want the same opportunity. So I simply explained to Miles how the vision had come about seven years earlier, how it had evolved to be based on the online medium, and what I saw as the potential for online to effect change in learning. I told the story chronologically, so he would understand the twists and turns. I made it clear that I was not a techie looking for another way to apply online technology, but rather was coming at it from the opposite direction—that I saw the Internet as simply another vehicle for delivering essential educational information to parents, such as how to help their kids get top grades, interact with teachers, determine if their child had a learning disability, and otherwise work the system. As usual, I was passionate about our mission. I had learned that passion is often important to investors in areas like education or health care, where there is a broader social mission at stake than just dollars and cents.

After an hour of conversation, Miles had heard enough. He stood up and said, "This is good. We need to get you down to AOL so you can meet Steve and Bob. You'll like them a lot." The touchdown buzzer went off in my head. I was ecstatic! Years of trying to get investors to take an interest in what we were doing and after just one hour, we had a meeting with Steve Case, the god of online and CEO of the savviest player on the Internet, and his second in command, Bob Pittman, to see if we could partner with them to build the education lane of that so-called information highway.

With that, Miles was out the door and on his way back to Dulles.

The Big Pitch

A month later, I was sitting together with two other members of my management team in a conference room at AOL's headquarters in Dulles, Virginia. Engaging us in small talk were Barry Schuler, who oversaw AOL's content offerings, George Vradenburg, AOL's top legal officer, who was enmeshed in trying to settle the many lawsuits from state attorneys general against AOL for its pricing practices, and two junior folks.

Suddenly, the door to the conference room swung open and in walked Steve Case and Bob Pittman to join us. The butterflies had left my stomach, only now my heart was thumping harder and faster than I could ever remember. Steve Case, *the* online visionary, had just walked in to have a meeting...with me and my soon-to-be-out-of-cash team! He looked like the preppy I had been led to expect, dressed in chinos and a button-down checked shirt. We had approximately 60 minutes to make our case. If we failed, we would probably be out of business. If we succeeded, we were on our way.

Then the all-important introductions. Miles as host launched in. "I think you all know why we're here. I met Jon a few weeks ago, through Ken (Novack, AOL's vice chairman), up in Boston and thought it would be a good idea if folks here could hear his story and meet some of his team." We then went around the room with the AOL folks giving very brief introductions and each of us giving essentially abbreviated biographies, which my team and I had rehearsed the night before—introductions that were not too long, but enough to strongly communicate credibility of experience. We wanted to signal that we had the mix of experiences to

take this market. First my two colleagues introduced
themselves.

Now the heads turned my way. I had outlined on a
notepad key points I wanted to emphasize as well as a list of
what I saw as our key assets. Off I went. "I'm the vision
guy," I started, "and I think there is a huge market
opportunity for AOL in education and that we are the partner
you want to play with." I then explained about how the
economy was quickly becoming knowledge-based and that
education was becoming increasingly critical to whether a
child would make it in today's world. While today this might
not be a great revelation, in 1997 this was not something we
ever took for granted in explaining our reason for being. I
also really felt that one of the most attractive aspects of our
company was the very bigness of the idea.

I explained that I thought education could be broken
into two segments, the supply side and the demand side. The
supply side was the schools, and there were a host of
entrenched competitors like McGraw Hill, Scholastic, and
Harcourt. The demand side (parents and their kids), however,
encompassed a third of our society and was up for grabs.
Moreover, that was where the dollars were—that there are
over 30 million households with kids under the age of
eighteen and "households with kids buy more stuff." I went
on to explain how education services could be a killer
retention application for AOL to lower member churn. Mid-
way through my monologue, Miles leaned over to our board
member who had made the original introduction, who was
sitting next to him, and whispered, "Boy, he can really get
going."

Next, I went through the strategy:

1. Go after the grass roots groups and get them to
    promote us to their members. They hate confusing
    their members and thus were unlikely to promote
    multiple services so in effect their was a mini land

grab underway for associate backing and we were way out in front.

2.   Focus on parents, and

3.   Run like mad to get schools to use our platform to build their school Web site so as to have a network of local Web sites that could connect parents to their kids' schools and to each other. I dropped in key developments, such as our recent initiative in Maryland, where a number of AOL executives lived and which had received wide publicity, as an example of winning the local school Web site landgrab.

Building Credibility

I wrapped up my presentation in about 20 minutes or so, to let the dialogue begin. It was essential for us to understand how the AOL folks were thinking about the education arena and how they reacted to our approach. Pittman was the first to speak. We had been led to believe that Pittman was tough, since he was AOL's new president and was known to be a super-aggressive businessman who valued money, power, and status over everything else. But we were surprised. His demeanor was soft and he was quite articulate. He signaled that a local school-by-school strategy made him nervous. His interest was in whether an approach such as ours could be rolled out nationally all at once.

Barry Schuler, who was the architect behind the AOL online mechanics, was really hard to gauge. He had this unsettling habit of not looking anyone in the eye during introductions and his body language was to be polite, standoffish. But he piped in that an education model could be scaled by "building community with our (AOL) tools". Frankly, I wasn't sure exactly what this meant as I had accessed several AOL parent chat rooms and been unable to see any that were compelling. In fact most were somewhat senseless and quickly lost their novelty. But I nodded anyway as a good salesman builds on positive acknowledgement.

Case said little during the course of the meeting, observing at one point, "We don't really need to make money on this." He left early, shortly after I completed my presentation, for his next meeting. Whew. At least he had gotten to hear my pitch.

Vradenburg, who was in the process of settling the lawsuits by consumer groups and more than a dozen state attorneys general, seemed extremely enthusiastic, and inquired about our relationships with PTA, the National School Boards Association, and other grass roots groups that might be helpful in his efforts. Luckily, we had just been invited by Vice President Gore to present at his annual "Family Reunion" conference held every year at Vanderbilt University in Nashville. Family Reunion convenes the senior public policy leaders on family public policy issues. This year Gore was focusing on the Internet. Vradenburg nodded approvingly when we explained our idea of working closely with public policy groups who were key influencers. We cited the example of the Maryland initiative for how this could help grow the business.

Finally, after about 90 minutes, Pittman, Schuler, and Vradenburg said they had to leave for another appointment, and the meeting came to a close. Miles signaled to his colleagues that he would get back to them to determine next steps, and we were done.

As we waited for a taxi to bring us back to Dulles airport, I was already flying high, though. I was buoyed on three fronts. First, Miles had delivered in terms of getting an audience with the right AOL folks. We had just presented to the most collectively high-powered group since we had begun the company. The fact that so many of AOL's most senior folks were there indicated that interest in the category from AOL was indeed high. This was good. Second, the overall tone was very positive. Other than Barry Schuler, who was hard to read, everyone seemed enthusiastic about the space and inclined to go forward. While there were no specifics discussed, it was clear that nobody had a clear sense of the education market and that one reason we had the audience we did was that we were perceived as knowing more than anyone else at AOL, and thus well positioned to educate AOL senior management. Lastly, we had accomplished our primary goal—to keep and build AOL's interest in us as its K-12 education partner.

As we headed out the door, Miles turned to me and said, "I'll circle back with folks and be in touch."

The Fruits of FEN's Labor

As dramatic as Jon's experience in attracting AOL's interest was, it was only the beginning. Those meetings merely set the stage for a complex and at times painful series of negotiations over many months. At one point, there was an agreement in principal for AOL to acquire FEN for $40 million cash and another $5 million of AOL stock. But AOL pulled out of the deal, leaving FEN's management temporarily dispirited.

Instead, FEN wound up with a consolation: a partnership whereby FEN became AOL's exclusive education content provider, expanding FEN's reach to millions of online parents. AOL acquired a 20% stake in the company (although its cash investment was negated by marketing fees FEN had to pay AOL for its privileged content dissemination role), obtained a seat on its board of directors, and provided it with an "executive in residence." While the arrangement didn't solve FEN's immediate cash problems, it did help position the fledgling company to raise more than $50 million of venture capital in 1999 and finally, in June 2000, to be acquired by Pearson, the huge British communication conglomerate, for $175 million cash. While the deal with Pearson was nothing to laugh at, it wound up netting Carson about 50% less than he would have with the original AOL acquisition offer, given the trajectory of AOL's stock.

Not only did Carson negotiate the partnership with AOL without the benefit of a written business plan, he also raised the $50 million of venture capital and completed the sale of the company to Pearson without the benefit of a full plan as well.

Key Ingredients

So how do you make key financing partnerships happen? Based on FEN's experience, along with those of other fledgling companies I have observed in recent years, it's a matter of putting together a number of components, which may vary in order of priority from situation to situation. But generally speaking, they include:

The right connections. For starters, you need to be able to get through to corporate decision makers who might be in a position to forge a partnership. While it can and sometimes does happen via cold-calling, more often than not it happens via having the right connections. Carson obtained his initial hearing before a key AOL executive because a member of his company's board of directors had a connection at AOL.

The right communication tools. Once upon a time, there was one key communication tool, and it was a written business plan. Today, as I've discussed in previous chapters, there are a number of important communication tools. Carson used several to advantage. He had his personal presentation down pat, along with a well-honed PowerPoint presentation he sometimes pulled out, depending on the audience. He also had an impressive Web site, enabling AOL executives to quickly and easily see what they might be getting. And he had used public relations to advantage, forging important relationships with credible nonprofit organizations like the PTA and maintaining a high profile in the education arena, making sure to get his company's accomplishments written up in the media.

The right package. When corporations begin looking around for potential small-company partners, it's usually because they have a specific and urgent need. And it's also because they have decided that the need is such that they don't want to invest the money and time in filling it internally. The small company that seems to fill that need gets the attention. AOL had in the case of FEN determined that it needed to develop a significant presence in the area of education. FEN had a complete education package for AOL at just the time when AOL was seeking such a package. For AOL, it was a make vs. buy decision. Should it spend much time and money building its own education outlet, or should it acquire the rights to use one that was already there? It was much more attractive to AOL to make use of what FEN had rather than build its own.

The right deal. Making a partnership with a major corporation actually happen typically takes a fair amount of negotiating. Even though a large company may be eager to acquire what your small company has, the terms won't necessarily be as attractive as you might expect. Entrepreneurs have a tendency to think that because large corporations have "deep pockets," they'll do whatever is necessary to make a partnership happen. Not so. Often the corporations will have scouted out several possible partner opportunities. They may negotiate with all of them, trying to obtain the best possible deal. It's up to entrepreneurs to try to anticipate what's really happening, and to determine what they're ready to give, and not give, in exchange for such a deal.

Once again, in all this discussion, there's been no mention of a written business plan. This isn't to say that some corporations wouldn't like to see a business plan, or even insist on one. But increasingly, it's not what makes these kinds of deals happen. What makes them happen is a total package of people, tools, promotion…and luck. ∎

Chapter 13

The Best Investor Relations Approach for You

CHAPTER SUMMARY

How to meet, impress and negotiate with investors in the most productive ways. Just as investors evaluate you, so should you protect your company and its value by evaluating prospective investors. Secure professional legal and financial advice for the all-important final negotiations involving valuation and price. Finally, you're ready to write a business plan.

"Focus on direct networking. I think broadcasting a business plan to a million people is a waste of everyone's time."
　　　　　　　　—*Venture capitalist participant in survey for this book*

T he process of dealing with investors is one of establishing and building relationships. The relationships must be nurtured over time. Occasionally it's a brief amount of time, a matter of a few weeks, but more often it's a matter of much longer amounts of time—many months, or even years.

My point in making this statement is to re-emphasize that there's no magic bullet in securing investment funds. Having a wonderful business plan won't do it for you any more than having a charming personality.

Having made the point that there's no magic bullet, I should note that some things you do can be more persuasive than others. As I explained in Chapter 10, nothing impresses investors quite as much as real sales, so building up a backlog of orders can have a huge impact on investors, and in combination with other things they've seen and liked about your company, can be the final factor that puts you over the top in their decision of whether or not to offer backing.

The situation isn't different in principal than what happens to publicly-held companies. Certain developments have a larger impact on stock prices than others. A company that records higher profits (usually based on higher sales) than professional securities analysts have projected typically sees its stock go up. News of a significant new customer order can also drive a company's stock price up. Likewise, negative news about profits or orders can drive investors to sell, which leads to a lower stock price.

So the question facing entrepreneurs is this: How do I meet, impress, and negotiate with investors to secure the funds I need? This chapter provides guidelines for doing all those things, and ends with considerations about developing a complete written business plan.

Meeting Investors

The main challenge in making the contacts with busy investors is that they are besieged by entrepreneurs like yourself. You put yourself in front of them via various techniques, including the following:

Focused networking. Networking is supposed to be the cure-all for entrepreneurs in search of investment funds. Go to enough entrepreneur investment conferences and presentation seminars that have become popular in major cities around the country, and you'll eventually meet investors interested in your company, goes the thinking.

Networking at such conferences tends to be random. Everyone wears name tags and you have to be in the right place at the right time to meet the investor who's likely right for you. Sometimes you'll hear an investor on a panel who seems to be appropriate for your business, and in such a case, you can approach the investor after the panel breaks up and give him or her a quick pitch and business card.

At some conferences, you can actually present your case to attending investors. A number of conferences are set up to allow entrepreneurs time to present—maybe three or five minutes each—and then interested investors seek out entrepreneurs of interest for further discussion. I have doubts about the effectiveness of this technique—based on the fact that entrepreneurs must often pay hundreds of dollars for the privilege of presenting, and the investors aren't necessarily screened for real interest. Investors themselves tend not to take these investor conferences very seriously. In my survey of venture capitalists, two-thirds of the 42 sampled said that investor conferences and business plan contests were either "not very" or "not at all" important to them. A reporter for *The Financial Times* wrote an account of one such conference in New York in early 2001, in which he concluded that the individuals making out best financially were the conference organizers.

I am a believer in networking, but I believe the networking needs to be highly focused. Some investor conferences are better than others—in terms of the quality and focus of the investors (by industry or size of company). A more targeted way to network is to use your existing contacts to obtain the names of prospective investors. Obtain names from your accountant and lawyer, and any other well-connected friends and relatives you can think of. Then you can use the existing contact to help you get through on the telephone to introduce yourself and determine potential interest.

Be ready with a pitch. Whether you are meeting prospective investors at a conference or via personal references, you want to have a ready pitch, sometimes referred to as "the elevator speech," ready to go. The idea here is to be able to present the high points of your company and the investment opportunity it affords in the time it takes to ride up the elevator of a high-rise office building with someone you've just met and wants to know about your company—typically about 30 seconds.

This elevator speech is something usually drawn from your presentation and/or synopsis—a brief description of the business and its main product or service, the size of the market, and the benefit for customers. Something like,

"We're making a new type of widget that will speed up packaging of potato chips and other snack foods by 50%. Snack foods, as you can imagine, represent a $20 billion market. Saving 50% on packaging translates into $100 million of savings. The snack food makers are very excited, to the extent that our product is already being used on a test basis by two major snack food producers."

Make your networking productive. Just because you are able to get an investor interested in speaking with you doesn't mean you've accomplished anything substantive. Investors are always on the lookout for interesting new companies, and also are interested in learning about the latest and greatest. So when they encounter someone they consider interesting, they'll sometimes try to learn as much as possible from the entrepreneurs about a topic area they find of interest. Before freely answering all their questions, try to pin them down as to what they are most interested in learning about and where they see the process going. Watch out for tire-kickers.

Try to protect yourself. Related to the previous point, don't be bashful about asking prospective investors to sign a non-disclosure statement. This one-to-two-page legal letter prohibits prospective investors from using information you consider proprietary. Many venture capitalists and other investor prospects won't sign them, for fear of legally compromising themselves if they decide to invest in one company after rejecting a company with a similar product or service. Even if they do sign, the reality is that there's no way to completely protect yourself from an unscrupulous individual who is determined to somehow use your intellectual property. But by asking prospective investors to agree not to divulge information about your venture, you are putting them on notice that you are protective of what's rightfully yours, and may take legal action that could prove both embarrassing and costly to violators.

Check out prospective investors. There is no reason you can't turn the tables and ask questions of potential investors. Look them up on the Internet. If their Web sites don't provide it, ask the investors which companies they've invested in over the last year. Feel free to ask questions like these: What kinds of situations most appeal to your firm? How many investments have you done in the last six months? What was the size range of the investments? How much time do you usually spend evaluating a promising new company? Do you have minimums or maximums about how much you'll invest? Are there industries you'd rather not get involved with? If something doesn't click or seem quite right, don't be afraid to end the relationship at an early stage.

Impressing Investors

Suppose at this point you have one or more investors interested in you, to the extent they are requesting followup information and sending someone around to ask questions of your executives. What is the best way to go forward so as to present yourself in the most favorable light?

Do things in the appropriate order for you. In other words, build on your strengths. If your business is heavily Web oriented, make sure to have a top-notch Web site completed. Then you'll feel comfortable saying, "The best way to be introduced to us and what we really do is to check out our Web site. You'll see a description of our company and its products, along with an area where we actually take orders." That puts the ball in the investor's court. If he or she hasn't reviewed the site and inquires, "Do you have some written material?" you can beg off and say, "I really think you should spend some time on our Web site. Then, I'll follow up with you and we can see what additional information you need." After you do follow up and determine that the Web site has done its job, you can offer to send your synopsis and/or financial summary.

Parcel out information. Related to the previous point, I'm a big believer in making information available in bite-sized chunks rather than all at once. In today's television-oriented environment, it's difficult to get anyone's attention for more than a few minutes at a time. If you send prospective investors a big package with your synopsis, copies of your slide presentation, your financial summary, and copies of all the articles that have been published in the media about your company, you run the risk of overwhelming the prospective investor.

Try for a personal meeting. As soon as possible during your courting, you want to get together in person, so you can make your PowerPoint presentation. A personal meeting can go much further than any printed or online material toward creating the "chemistry" that is so essential to winning investors over to your viewpoint. Similarly, an absence of chemistry or feelings of discomfort on either side can end the relationship and prevent it from dragging on unproductively.

Keep the information coming. If your relationship with prospective investors is typical and you have one or two who have expressed serious interest, you'll need to figure out ways to stay in front of them. One excellent way to do that is via regular written updates, almost like a newsletter of developments. The best kind of update to provide is news about new customers and orders, especially if the customers are well known, like corporations, and the orders are sizable. You can also report on new hires, product or service enhancements, and other signs of progress. Short punchy email messages updating prospective investors can help shift the tide in your favor when they are possibly vacillating.

Think about how publicly-held companies handle investor relations. They hire professionals or engage outside agencies to feed information—via press releases, conference calls, and white papers—to the investment community of mutual funds, stock brokers, pension funds, and others. They take these costly steps because they want to keep investors interested in buying their companies' stocks. You want to do the same thing.

Negotiating Effectively

Just because you get investors to say yes, they want to invest in you, doesn't mean you have the money. As the previous chapter's case study made clear, you nearly always need to go through a few significant steps yet, and at any one of them, the potential deal could unravel. Remember, while both you and investors have in common the desire to make a lot of money, you also have important differences in perspective. While you want to obtain as much investment funding as possible while giving up as little as possible, investors want just the opposite—to provide as little funding as possible in exchange for as much of your company as possible. Here are some steps you should take:

Evaluate the investors. Learn from other entrepreneurs who have dealt with this firm or firms (if multiple investor groups are involved) about their modus operandi. Ask for the names of other companies the investors have backed and interview the executives of those companies to learn about their experiences in working with the investors, and about their investment style. Did they do everything they promised? How involved have they been since providing the investment funds? Are their questions and requests reasonable? Are they inclined toward replacing top management at the first sign of trouble? Different investors have different personalities, and as much as you may want and need investment funds, don't let that blind you to the potential "investor from hell."

To the extent that you understand how they operate, you'll be able to anticipate their moves, and make well-informed decisions about whether to continue on a path with one or another of them.

Understand the contingencies. Investment deals tend not to be straightforward. Sometimes you'll at long last hear this opening line: "We'll invest if…" They may say they'll put in some part of the money, but you have to find other investors to do the rest. Depending on how such a contingency is structured, it can be a positive or a negative.

If it's structured very specifically—as in "We'll give you $1 million of the $3 million you need, once you find investors ready to put up $2 million more"—you can use the $1 million commitment to help attract additional money. But if it's structured more vaguely—"We're interested in investing, but we want to see other investors become interested as well before we make a decision"—then the commitment isn't much help, because it suggests to other investors a less than wholehearted interest.

Be prepared to agonize about price. Actually negotiating an investment deal most fundamentally involves establishing a price the investors will pay for your company's stock. The core decision entrepreneurs who attract investor interest are faced with invariably is determining whether the price is fair. In the recent high-anxiety investor atmosphere, entrepreneurs have increasingly been deciding that the price isn't fair. In some cases, investors are offering prices that entrepreneurs consider unconscionably low, and they are turning investors down. A low stock price means that investors must acquire more of your company for you to get the total amount of funds you need. Thus, investors might offer you the $3 million you are after, but demand 80% of the stock rather than the 40% you were expecting to part with. It all goes back to valuation, which I discussed in Chapter 12.

Obtain your own legal and financial advice. Once you begin to talk specifically about terms of a possible investment, it is absolutely essential that you obtain the advice of at least one professional with legal and business expertise. Remember, the investors negotiate such transactions all the time, and thus understand the nuances of such agreements much better than you ever will, since you are doing it for probably the first time. Ideally, your adviser should be a lawyer with extensive experience negotiating investment deals on behalf of entrepreneurs. Growing numbers of lawyers have come to specialize in working with fast-growing companies. They know the ins and outs of the negotiating process and the terms common in such agreements. They can tell you what is routine, and what is excessive or unorthodox. These people aren't inexpensive, but the stakes are high enough that you need to bite the bullet and make the commitment.

And What About That Plan?

As I have stated at several points, I am arguing for smart planning and prioritizing—that there are usually other steps entrepreneurs should take before becoming wrapped up in preparing a business plan. I am making that argument based on how professional investors have come to treat the business plan.

While professional investors still place value in a complete written business plan, most don't place a huge amount of value in it, especially in comparison to other practices. In my survey, a clear majority, 62% of respondents, said the business plan was only "somewhat" important in their overall evaluation of a business, while a vocal minority, 36%, said it was "very" important.

And if you'll recall, I pointed out that 88% said they will listen to an oral presentation from a company that hasn't completed a full written business plan. Then I followed up with those who said they would listen to the presentation, and asked this question: "If the presentation leads you to want to invest, will you insist on the preparation of a complete business plan before completing the funding?" Here, the respondents split nearly down the middle, with 51% saying they would insist on a plan, and 49% saying they wouldn't.

The implication here is important. First, the investors are clearly saying that having a written business plan in place at the start of the evaluation process isn't essential. Second, they are saying that even later, after an investment decision has been made, a business plan may or may not be essential. Not an overwhelming endorsement for driving yourself crazy to write a plan.

With all that being said, I would advise entrepreneurs to expect to develop a complete written plan at some point in the process—more than likely near or at the end of the investment process rather than at the beginning. For guidance on that process, I refer you to Appendix III of this book, "What All Business Plans Must Cover" and, for more detail, one of two books I've written: *Business Plans That Win $$$: Lessons from the MIT Enterprise Forum* (coauthored with Stanley Rich, published by HarperCollins) or *How to Really Create a Successful Business Plan* (Inc. Publishing).

Remember, a written business plan is just one component of a larger process of managing and growing your business. The issues that come up are constantly changing, and your challenge is to keep your eye on the right issues at the right time. It's more essential to plan the business than it is to write a business plan. ■

Appendix I

Summary of Professional Investor Research

This study was carried out in February 2002. It was conducted using email to direct respondents to an online questionnaire. Emails were sent to 360 partners of small business investment companies (SBICs), which are venture capital and private equity firms that receive some of their capital via the U.S. Small Business Administration; some 42 agreed to participate in the survey, for a response rate of 12%.

Here are the main questions, and the response percentages:

I have invested in one or more businesses during the past three years without the benefit of having reviewed a complete business plan (15-40 pages)
Yes: 43%
No: 57%

If you answered yes to the previous question, what percentage of the companies you've invested in over the past three years have been done without the benefit of a complete business plan?
Less than one-fourth: 84%
One-fourth to one-half: 16%

To what extent do business plans you see provide a clear and accurate assessment of the company's current operations and likely prospects for the future?
Great extent: 10%
Modest extent: 74%
Poor extent: 17%

How important is a written business plan in your overall evaluation of a business?

Very:	36%
Somewhat:	62%
Not very:	2%

I can become intrigued by a company that I am referred to by reliable sources, even if it doesn't yet have a complete written business plan.

Yes:	98%
No:	2%

How do you ideally prefer to learn about a promising investment candidate?

An entrepreneur sends me a business plan over
the transom: 2%
I am referred to a company or an entrepreneur is referred to
me by someone whose judgment I trust—a colleague,
professional, friend, etc.: 96%
Other (networking, online investigation, etc.) 2%
I meet an entrepreneur at an investment or trade
conference: 0%

Will you listen to an oral presentation from founders of a company that is especially intriguing to you, even if they haven't completed a full business plan?

Yes:	88%
No:	12%

If you answered yes to the previous question—if the presentation leads you to want to invest, will you insist on the preparation of a complete business plan before completing funding?

Yes:	51%
No:	49%

How important are formal get-togethers—like investor conferences or business plan contests—in helping you discover serious investment candidates?

Very:	0%
Somewhat:	33%
Not very:	52%
Not at all:	14%

Since the events of September 11, 2001, my investment approach has changed as follows:

I've become more cautious about making investments:	24%
I've become less cautious:	0%
I haven't changed:	76%

The most significant shortcomings in the business plans I see are (respondents checked as many as applied; top five included):

Financial projections too far removed from reality (either optimistic or pessimistic):	81%
Not clearly written—too much lingo and hype:	67%
Insufficient explanation of business model:	52%
Failure to demonstrate customer interest:	50%
Don't provide enough information about current state of business:	45%

Appendix II
Research Study of Business Planning

Does Formal Business Planning Enhance the Performance of New Ventures?

G.T. Lumpkin, University of Illinois at Chicago
Rodney C. Shrader, University of Illinois at Chicago
Gerald E. Hills, University of Illinois at Chicago

This study was published in the 1998 *Frontiers of Entrepreneurship Research*, which includes all research papers presented at the annual Babson College-Kauffman Entrepreneurship Research Conference. Included here is the Abstract and Introduction of the study, followed by a link to the Babson College web page containing the full study.

Abstract

The importance of planning to performance is a central premise in the entrepreneurship and strategic management literature. The business plan is regard by many as an essential element of a successful start-up; ongoing planning efforts are considered vital to continued success. Empirical investigations of established firms, however, have generally been unable to find a strong link between business planning and performance. Is the planning—performance relationship also tenuous among new venture firms? This study examined the planning—performance link among 54 new entrant and 40 established firms. Results suggest that the types of planning that may contribute to performance change as firms age, and that planning may not need to be in the form of a written business plan.

Introduction

Conventional wisdom and anecdotal evidence appear to take it for granted that planning positively influences firm performance (Roberts, 1983). Some scholars have concluded that lack of planning or poor planning may lead to firm failure (Robinson & Pearce, 1983). Furthermore, venture capitalists report that a majority of entrepreneurs could avoid failure through better analysis of external circumstances (Hills, 1984). For these reasons, emphasis on business planning and analysis abounds within the realm of entrepreneurship.

Unfortunately, empirical findings indicate that, among established firms, the planning-performance relationship is not as straightforward as conventional wisdom suggests. In fact, findings have been so contradictory that some scholars have called the planning-performance relationship tenuous (e.g., Pearce, Freeman & Robinson, 1987), concluded that planning may not be necessary at all (e.g., Shuman, Sussman, & Shaw, 1985), or argued that planning may actually hinder firm performance (e.g., Thurston, 1983). However, following a critical review of the literature (Pearce, et al., 1987) and a meta-analysis (Schwenk & Shrader, 1993), scholars have argued that firm size and stage of development are critical factors in understanding the link between planning and performance.

In fact, they concluded that failure to consider these factors has contributed to the contradictory and counter-intuitive findings of previous studies. Indeed, after controlling for size by conducting a meta-analysis of only small firm studies, Schwenk and Shrader (1993) found a positive, although modest, planning-performance relationship across studies. They concluded that the question is no longer "does strategic planning affect small firm performance?" but rather "under what conditions is performance enhanced by small firm strategic planning?" One such condition, they proposed, is the stage of firm development. These and other scholars argue that, given their more limited resources, young and small firms are more likely to enhance performance through informal application of strategic decision-making practices than through formal business planning (Lindsay & Rue, 1980; Pearce et al. 1987; Robinson & Pearce, 1983; Schwenk & Shrader, 1993). As McGrath and MacMillan (1995) point out, there are fundamental differences between planning for new ventures, which are more likely to rely on unproved assumptions, and planning for established lines of business with a track record to consult.

Given the proposed relationship between planning and performance, and the proposed moderating influences of firm size and stage of development, this study examines the link between planning (both formal and informal) and performance in a group of new and established small firms. Three important questions are addressed: (1) Is business planning and analysis important to success? (2) Does it matter whether that planning is formal or informal? (3) Does the relationship between business planning and performance differ between new entrants and established firms?

For the full study, go to:
http://www.babson.edu/entrep/fer/papers98/VII/VII_A/VII_A.ht

Appendix III

What All Business Plans Must Cover

Here is a brief overview of the contents of a written business plan. Keep in mind that after the first two items, the titles of the subsequent sections can vary. But every business plan should cover the subjects addressed in this overview:

- **Cover Page.** On the cover page goes the name of your company, its address and phone number, and the chief executive's name. This may seem obvious, but it's amazing how many business plans don't have a cover page or have an incomplete one. If the plan is going to be distributed to several bankers or investors, you will want to number each plan prominently on the cover page—to allow you to track the plans and to inhibit recipients from copying or widely passing around the plan. (You should also have recipients sign a nondisclosure statement).
- **Table of Contents.** This should include a logical arrangement of the sections of your business plan, with page numbers. Once again, this is something that seems obvious, but many business plans are put together with content pages and no page numbers.
- **Executive Summary.** This is the heart of the business plan. It is not an abstract or a list of ideas. It is really the business plan in miniature, and thus is the most difficult section to write.
- **The Company.** The business plan must provide basic information about the company: its past, present, and future. That is, there should be information about the company's history or, if it's a start-up, about the evolution of the market and product concept. Information is necessary as well about the company's current status. And what is the company's future

strategy? What are its goals and what actions are required to achieve its goals?

- **The Market.** This is your assessment of the customer groups you've targeted, other customer groups you might pursue, the competition, and marketing efforts thus far. Is the market growing, how fast is it growing, and what evidence do you have that it is interested in your product or service?
- **The Product/Service.** Here is where you describe your product and/or service and what makes it special and attractive. What are the components of the product/service? How much do you charge? What services don't you provide? What kind of warranty do you provide and what are its particular provisions?
- **Sales and Promotion.** This is your assessment of how you intend to carry out your marketing plan—how you'll reach your customers and sell to them. Do you have an in-house sales force or will you use manufacturer's representatives, direct mail, or contracted telemarketers to sell your product/service? What kind of public relations do you have planned? Will it be done internally or will you hire a public relations firm?
- **Finances.** Here is where you detail your past results, if there are any, and your expectations for the future. This section should include cash flow projections, profit-and-loss statements, and balance sheets. All the figures should be cast in traditional accounting format.
- **Risks and Opportunities.** You should identify potential problems that could interfere with the company's success, or delay key milestones. These might include competitive issues, failure to obtain a patent, or delays in production.
- **Appendix.** This is for important documents that are too lengthy to be included in the main business plan, such as resumés of the management team, advertisements, and product specifications.

Index